CHRISTIAN LIBERTY

A New Testament Perspective

CHRISTIAN LIBERTY

A New Testament Perspective

James D. G. Dunn

WILLIAM B. EERDMANS PUBLISHING COMPANY
GRAND RAPIDS, MICHIGAN

First published 1993 by the Paternoster Press
P.O. Box 300, Carlisle, Cumbria, CA3 0QS, UK

This edition published 1994
through special arrangement with Paternoster by
Wm. B. Eerdmans Publishing Co.
255 Jefferson Ave. S.E., Grand Rapids, Michigan 49503

00 99 98 97 96 95 94   7 6 5 4 3 2 1

Library of Congress Cataloging-in-Publication Data

Dunn, James D. G., 1939-
Christian liberty: a New Testament perspective / James D. G. Dunn.
p.   cm.
Includes bibliographical references and indexes.
ISBN 0-8028-0796-8 (paper)
1. Liberty — Religious aspects — Christianity. I. Title.
BT810.2.D86   1994
261.7′2 — dc20   94-16688
CIP

In memory of

Bob Guelich
(1940–91)

a soul-knit friend
(1 Sam. 18:1)
and fellow-inquirer
after the truth of the gospel
now rejoicing in
'the glorious liberty
of the children of God'
(Rom. 8:21)

Contents

Preface

The theme of Christian liberty is one on which I have reflected for many years. It was a major interest during my postgraduate studies in Cambridge in the 1960s. As those whose earlier Christian experience had been in more conservative circles, it was an important existential issue for Meta (my wife) and me. To what extent was a Christian free in discussing critical questions to reach controversial conclusions? To what extent were Christians free to question long established traditions of ecclesiastical order or the unwritten conventions which governed life-style and the pattern of social relationships? To what extent were Christians free to explore new and different ways to speak and live the gospel? Was liberty a threat to faith or one of its prime expressions?

This was the middle '60s and the unrest which boiled up to the student revolution of 1968 was already stirring. How could one be in a dynamic student community and not be aware of it or be unaffected by it? Our own group of aspiring New Testament PhDs and their spouses wrestled with many aspects of critical thought, but the issue of Christian liberty was particularly prominent as a topic of burning personal interest in our friendships with Rob and Julie Banks. Several of the points made in the following pages had their first airing in a conversation which began nearly thirty years ago and is still going strong.

When the invitation came to deliver the 1991 Didsbury Lectures at the Nazarene Theological College, Manchester, therefore, it was the theme of Christian Liberty which came to me as an appropriate subject. The opportunity to extend my reading and reflections on the topic at least a little further and to organise my thoughts into somewhat clearer order was too good to miss. And in a day when the forces of fundamentalism are gathering strength once again on all sides, the theme of Liberty, and not least Christian Liberty, is one to which attention must needs be given, else it will be strangled by the chains of simplistic certainties bound and padlocked by legalistic thought police.

The days spent in Manchester for the Lectures were very pleasant ones, giving rise to several interesting discussions and conversations, once again with existential 'bite'; how could it be otherwise with this as the theme? I am most grateful to the Revd. H. McGonigle, Principal of the Nazarene Theological College, for the invitation to give the Lectures, and to his colleagues, Dr Kent Brower in particular, for their fine hospitality in those November days.

At the time I coupled the name of Bob Guelich with those of the two great Manchester biblical scholars, Fred Bruce and Barnabas Lindars, both of whom had died recently. But it was the death, so untimely as it appears from a human perspective, of Bob Guelich which was the greatest shock. He was not part of the Cambridge group, but was wholly one with its spirit and became a cherished friend of its various members in the following years. It was a particular delight to Meta and me that Rob Banks and Bob Guelich came together latterly in the same institution (Fuller Theological Seminary), and that our last memory of Bob is of a glorious evening we all spent together in Pasadena in the summer of 1990. Next year in Jerusalem, for 'the Jerusalem above is free' (Gal. 4:26).

James D.G. Gunn
University of Durham
July, 1993

CHAPTER ONE

What is Liberty?

1. Introduction

Liberty is an ideal of which no one disapproves. It is essentially something positive, a 'good' which many might wish to qualify but none to deny. It is a word which stirs the heart and fires the imagination as few other words do. It has roused slumbering nations and united the most diverse of opinions in a common cause. It has inspired poets and statesmen to some of the loftiest sentiments ever penned. It has braced the courage and resolve of many a martyr in the hour of undeserved death.

Who, for example, can fail to resonate with the words of Patrick Henry, a leading figure in the American war of Independence and in the articulation of the American rights: 'I know not what course others may take; but as for me, give me liberty, or give me death'? Or with the ideals of the French Revolution still impressed on French coins: 'Liberty, Equality, Fraternity'. Or with Byron's romantic self-identification with the liberation of Greece?[1] –

---

1 Lord Byron, 'Don Juan' III.86.3.

> The mountains look on Marathon –
> And Marathon looks on the sea;
> And musing there an hour alone,
> I dream'd that Greece might still be free.

Returning across the Atlantic, we may simply recall the popular national anthem of the United States:

> My country, 'tis of thee,
> Sweet land of liberty,
> Of thee I sing:
> Land where my fathers died,
> Land of the pilgrims' pride,
> From every mountain-side
> Let freedom ring

Nor can we forget the way Martin Luther King was able to draw on the same vision and ideal in our own time in one of the most powerful expressions of the longing for liberty of an oppressed people.[2]

It is this idealization of freedom which lies at the heart of all the great charters of the western world: the Magna Carta (1215), with its guarantee of freedom for the church and its documentation by King John of the liberties of all free men in the kingdom 'to be had and held by them and their heirs of us and our heirs'; the American Declaration of Independence (1776), with its ringing opening, 'We hold these truths to be self-evident, that all men are created equal, that they are endowed by their Creator with certain unalienable Rights, that among these are Life, Liberty and the pursuit of Happiness'; and the Universal Declaration of Human Rights (1948) with its masterly setting out of fundamental human freedoms, including freedom of speech and belief and freedom from fear and want, and its echo of the similar aspirations of the French Revolution in its opening article, 'All human beings are born free and equal in dignity and rights.'

---

2 Speech in Washington DC, 27.8.63.

The same language and ideal lie at the heart of the biblical and Christian traditions. The Jewish scriptures (the OT) can be said to be largely circumscribed round the two foci of the Exodus and the return from Exile. Israel was never allowed to forget that its history as God's people began as the liberation of an enslaved people. So, for example, in what we might call the earliest declaration of human rights and responsibilities, the Ten Commandments, we recall the opening words: 'I am the Lord your God, who brought you out of the land of Egypt, out of the house of slavery.' In Isa. 61:1 the prophet no doubt has in mind the return from the Babylonian captivity when he writes the much quoted passage:

> The spirit of the Lord God is upon me,
> because the Lord has anointed me;
> he has sent me to bring good news to the oppressed,
> to bind up the brokenhearted,
> to proclaim liberty to the captives,
> and release to the prisoners.

The Christian scriptures in turn contain the same passage applied by Jesus to his own mission (Luke 4:18) and such words as those of the Johannine Jesus – 'You will know the truth, and the truth will make you free. . . . So if the Son makes you free, you will be free indeed' (John 8:32, 36). Nor may we forget the fundamental importance of Christian liberty for Paul, as illustrated by the impassioned appeal to the Galatians, 'For freedom Christ has set us free; stand fast therefore, and do not submit again to the yoke of slavery' (Gal. 5:1). And Christian tradition can justly boast of that quintessential exposition of the spirit of the Reformation, Martin Luther's 'The Freedom of a Christian', with its double proposition and paradox: 'A Christian is a perfectly free lord of all, subject to none.

A Christian is a perfectly dutiful servant of all, subject to all.'[3]

Here then is a concept and ideal which we might think has universal approbation and one worthy of our considered reflection. On the other hand, a subject so universally approved must surely be rather dull – a tiresome recital of what we all agree on anyway. It comes as rather a shock, therefore, and perhaps we should confess, something of a relief, to recall that liberty has not always been perceived as such an unmixed blessing, and certainly the ideal is to be seen more by the eye of the visionary than in the real world. I was half minded, had I the time, to read the whole text of the Universal Declaration of Human Rights, all thirty articles, so obvious would it be that its terms are so little known and so widely disregarded.

Instead, let me simply remind you that for all the praise heaped on 'liberty', its close associates 'liberal' and 'liberalism' have often received a very different press – even though one would have thought that a 'liberal', by definition, was one who maintained the several causes of 'liberty'. Perhaps the classic expression of hostility to liberalism in the theological arena (though not only there) was provided by John Henry Newman, when he defended his description of 'liberalism' as 'the Anti-dogmatic Principle'.[4]

> Liberty of thought is in itself a good; but it gives an opening to false liberty. Now by Liberalism I mean false liberty of thought, or the exercise of thought upon matters, in which, from the constitution of the human mind, thought cannot be brought to any successful issue, and therefore is out of place. Among such matters

---

3 Accessible e.g. in J. Dillenberger, *Martin Luther. Selections from his writings* (Garden City, New York: Doubleday, Anchor Books, 1961) pp. 52–85, here p. 53.
4 *Apologia Pro Vita Sua*, ed. M. J. Svaglic (Oxford: Clarendon, 1967) pp. 254–62, here pp. 255–6.

are first principles of whatever kind; and of these the
most sacred and momentous are especially to be
reckoned the truths of Revelation. Liberalism then is
the mistake of subjecting to human judgment those
revealed doctrines which are in their nature beyond and
independent of it, and of claiming to determine on
intrinsic grounds the truth and value of propositions
which rest for their reception simply on the external
authority of the Divine Word.

Despite Newman, 'Liberalism', of course, gave its name
to a whole epoch of theological history which lasted
well into this century. But the horrors of the first
European war seemed to demonstrate to most that
liberalism's reaction against external authority had
gone too far and its faith in human motivation and
morality had been proved unrealistic and over-
optimistic beyond dispute. In political and theological
circles stretching far beyond the circle of Newman's
followers 'liberalism' became a bad word, the slogan of
a discredited minority. Typical of current sentiment
stretching far beyond theological circles, is the way in
which George Bush running for President of the United
States in 1988, was able to castigate and defeat his
opponent, Michael Dukakis, by labelling him with the
big 'L' word. How deeply ironic that in the country
symbolized by the Statue of Liberty in New York
harbour, 'liberal' should become a word which smears
and discredits a candidate for its presidency.

The topic then has more appeal than might at first
have appeared. For Liberty is an ideal at the heart of
the western democratic tradition and, in particular, at
the heart of Jewish and Christian self-understanding.
But it is an ideal more honoured in the breach than in
the observance. And it is an ideal which in its
implementation in liberal thought and action has been
profoundly questioned and widely rejected. What then
is liberty? Is it simply an unreal ideal, orphan child of

Jean-Jacques Rousseau's vision of a golden age of primeval society in which all were free and equal?[5] Or is it an ideal still to be held before humanity? More to the point, is liberty an ideal which can be experienced in the here and now? Or are the experiences of liberation, so heady and intoxicating in the moment of release, always fated to turn to dust and ashes in the mouth before their taste has been full savoured? Is the hope of real liberty always to be disappointed and frustrated by human weakness, greed and folly? Is liberalism always to be distrusted and held suspiciously at arm's length lest it open the floodgates to anarchy and the rule of naked might?

Such are the questions in mind as we launch forth on this series of lectures on Christian liberty. I do so tentatively, since I have no expertize in most of the broad areas of the humanities over which the subject of liberty stretches and have no wish to isolate the theme of Christian liberty from the broader theme of which it is a part. It is important, I would agree, that any discussion of Christian liberty should show itself at least aware of these broader areas, otherwise the Christian understanding of the theme will appear narrowly introverted, and its potential contribution to broader studies and larger aspirations be disqualified from the start. However, I must be realistic, and in these lectures all I can hope to do is to offer some preliminary reflections on the larger theme of liberty before turning to three case studies in the New Testament, the area of my own specialism. To concentrate such a large subject into such a small area will inevitably make for a more limited discussion than the

---

5 According to Rousseau, writing in 1755, man 'in the state of nature' had been 'free, healthy, honest and happy', but had been corrupted and enslaved by the growth of social institutions (see e.g. *Encyclopedia Britannica* IV.657).

subject requires. However, since I take seriously the status of the NT writings as in effect the constitutional expressions of and safeguards for Christian liberty, I entertain some hope that the discussion despite its limited base will have wider value.

Let me begin by offering some definitions before attempting further analysis.

2. Basic definitions

It is hardly an exaggeration to say that the Western idea of liberty is rooted in the free cities of ancient Greece. Fundamental to Greek self-perception was the thought of freedom. 'The Greek finds his personal dignity in the fact that he is free.'[6] And that meant precisely, free and not a slave. It is this relation to and contrast with slavery which first defines freedom.

The point was that a slave was not his own master. As a generalization we can say that slaves had some, limited, rights. But the basic fact of life was that they were at the disposal of others. In the generally accepted definition given by Aristotle, the slave is one who by nature (that is, by the nature of enslavement) belongs not to himself but to someone else.[7] This, we should perhaps remind ourselves, was not yet considered a moral issue. Slavery was universally accepted as a normal social institution and economic fact of life. Slavery was regarded as a misfortune, but not as a wrong in itself. Nevertheless there was a clear line marked between the slave and the free person, and the citizen of a free Greek city could never regard the status of the slave with anything but abhorrence. Nor was slavery limited to the lowest jobs in society; there were

---

6 K. H. Rengstorf, *TDNT* 2.261.
7 Aristotle, *Pol.*, 1.2 p. 1254a, 14 (*TDNT* 2.487–8).

free men who laboured with their hands, and slaves who held secretarial and managerial positions.[8] The essence of slavery, however, was subjection to the will of another. For example, it was almost unknown in classical antiquity to find a freeman as a personal servant; for it was being subject to another man's orders which was considered servile and degrading.

We can see something of what liberty meant from the various decrees of manumission which have been uncovered, describing the transition from slavery to freedom. These indicate that there were four rights which manumission regularly conferred: first, 'legal status as a protected member of the community'; second, 'immunity from arbitrary arrest'; third, the 'right to work at whatever he desires to do'; and fourth, 'the right to movement according to his own choice'.[9] Freedom therefore was essentially freedom to decide for oneself, what one wanted to do, where one wanted to go, under the protection of the normal rights of the citizen.

We should pause at this point to note an immediate corollary of far reaching significance in relation to our opening remarks. For as freedom is defined in antithesis to slavery, so the antithesis of 'liberal' is not 'conservative', but 'servile' or slavish. In classical terms the essence of liberty is not freedom from older systems or traditional values, but freedom from slavish obedience, that is, from obedience determined by legal status of bondage and not by the quality of relationship or the merits of the case. The antithesis of liberal and conservative is a much later development born of the Renaissance and the Enlightenment.

---

8 See D. B. Martin, *Slavery as Salvation. The Metaphor of Slavery in Pauline Christianity* (New Haven: Yale University, 1990).
9 W. L. Westermann, 'Between Slavery and Freedom', *American Historical Review* 50 (1945) pp. 213–27, cited by F. A. Hayek, *The Constitution of Liberty* (London: Routledge & Kegan Paul, 1960) pp. 19–20.

In classical antiquity, however, this basic concept of liberty, as freedom from slavery, was extended or developed in two directions. Firstly it was developed in the larger concept of *political* freedom. In the Greek understanding of the state, freedom was indispensable. It was of the essence of the fledgling democracy of the free Greek states that their citizens should be able to determine their own laws. This also meant, conversely, that freedom was understood as freedom within the law, freedom under the law so determined. The ideal and practice of freedom was also shaped by the city states' struggles for freedom from tyranny, whether the arbitrary and inordinate claims of a single tyrant, or the potential tyranny of the Persians. Hence the idealization of such heroes as Harmodius and Aristogiton, and of Leonidas, the hero of Thermopylae.[10] The ideal is again the same: defence of *eleutheria*, the freedom of a city and its citizens, is defence of *autonomia*, the freedom of a state to make and live within its own laws.

The second way in which the basic metaphor of freedom from slavery was elaborated was in terms of what we would now call *personal* freedom, or inner freedom. For the more thoughtful were fully aware that there were slaveries other than those imposed by the might of external force. As Philo, the first century Jewish philosopher, notes,[11]

> Slavery is applied in one sense to bodies, in another to souls; bodies have men for their masters, souls their vices and passions. The same is true of freedom; one freedom produces security of the body from men of superior strength, the other sets the mind at liberty from the domination of the passions.

---

10 Details in *Oxford Classical Dictionary*, ed. N. G. L. Hammond & H. H. Scullard (Oxford: Clarendon, 1970) pp. 112 and 595.
11 Quod Omnis Probus Liber Sit (Every Good Man is Free) 17.

What it was that made a man truly free was a subject much debated in Cynic and Stoic circles. By his disavowal of the world the Cynic could claim to be truly free, for he was no longer dependent on the world for satisfaction. And by disengagement from his passions and from dependence on their fulfilment the Stoic sought to be free, even from the fear of death.

These two aspects of liberty, civil or political liberty, and inner or spiritual freedom, have dominated all subsequent reflection on the theme. The only really new factor has been in effect the merging of the two as a result of the rise of individualism in the modern world – that is, the emergence of the idea of *individual* liberty as a conscious *political* ideal. For despite the eccentric individualism of a Diogenes,[12] or the tragic independent spirit of an Antigone, the notion of individual rights as such seems not to have featured in the legal discussions of the Greco-Roman world. 'The sense of privacy itself', claims Isaiah Berlin, 'of the area of personal relationships as something sacred in its own right, derives from a conception of freedom which, for all its religious roots, is scarcely older, in its developed state, than the Renaissance or the Reformation.'[13] Be that as it may, the idea of the liberty of the individual has become one of the most important features in discussions on freedom over the past two hundred years, the classic statement being, I suppose, John Stuart Mill's essay *On Liberty*.[14]

These three features of traditional and more recent studies of freedom suggest the outline for our own reflections: first on liberty and authority, then on liberty and the self, and finally liberty and society.

---

12 See *Oxford Classical Dictionary* p. 348.
13 I. Berlin, *Four Essays on Liberty* (London: Oxford University, 1969) p. 129.
14 J. S. Mill, *On Liberty* (1859); I have used the Penguin Classics edition (Harmondsworth, 1985).

3. Liberty and authority

Central to any discussion of liberty is the tension between freedom and authority. The paradox of liberty is that it is experienced quintessentially as freedom *from*, and yet it is fundamentally unstable and unsustainable as such. It is experienced as freedom from constraint, from rule, from law; and yet without constraint, without rule, without law it cannot survive. A few illustrations should help to explain what I mean.

At the heart of the concept of liberty is the emotional experience of being liberated. If freedom is by basic definition the opposite of slavery, then the high point of liberty for anyone who has known slavery is the moment of liberation. This presumably is why heroes like Harmodius, Aristogiton and Leonidas were so celebrated. They symbolized in themselves the decisive action by which liberation was achieved (the slaying of the tyrant), or defended (against the overwhelming odds of the Persians). Similarly in biblical history, the Exodus gains a mythical symbolical power of incalculable force, as the event, the decisive transition from bondage to the status of a free people, which characterizes Israel's self-understanding, as a people chosen by God for himself alone and not for anything that they were.[15]

So also in modern times the Liberty Bell in Philadelphia, with its motto, 'Proclaim liberty throughout all the land unto all the inhabitants thereof' (Lev. 25:10), is prized in the United States, since it symbolizes the moment of independence – the legend being that it was rung on July 4, 1776, to signal the Congress' adoption of the Declaration of Independence. In France, Delacroix's famous painting captures the same

---

15 For the influence of the Exodus in OT writings see e.g. *Anchor Bible Dictionary*, ed. D. N. Freedman (New York: Doubleday, 1992) 2.701.

symbolism in its depiction of bare-breasted Liberty leading her people to freedom against the oppression of the old order.[16] The same sense of the significant moment, the *kairos*, is evident in the fact that so many Liberation Movements in the world have named themselves after some particularly crucial date, or Governments have decreed public holidays on the date when independence was achieved — all attempts to harness the emotional power of that moment of liberation to sustain national bonding. So presumably in years ahead, future generations will look back to November 9th, 1989, and try to relive the heady excitement of the day when the Berlin Wall was decisively breached.

The trouble is, of course, that that heady moment of liberation soon passes, and what then? The freedman would almost certainly find himself in a client-patron relationship which in its own way was as restrictive of his liberty as his former slavery. The Greek city states found all too often that fledgling democracy all too easily gives way to a new form of oligarchy and tyranny, or resolves itself into a different form of tyranny, the tyranny of the majority. Nor need I remind you of how the ideals of the French Revolution quickly gave way to the horrors of the Reign of Terror, of how in the present century the independence or former colonies soon revealed their more fundamental dependence on an economic and world order where the rules were determined by others, or of how quickly the hopes of new liberty in eastern Europe are being dashed by resurgent aggressive nationalisms.

Similar illustrations could, of course, be developed at the level of the individual. Archetypal here is the transition from minority to majority, including the awakening of sexual instincts and appetite on the one hand, and typically also the opening of the windows of

---

16 Exhibited at the Louvre, Paris.

the mind to new vistas of knowledge on the other. To witness or participate in the adolescent's liberation from unquestioned axioms into inquiring self-awareness is one of the joys experienced by the university teacher. At the same time, no university tutor would have difficulty in recalling cases where freedom from the constraints of childhood has had catastrophic effects. There are aspects of this to which we will have to return shortly. Here it is the tension between liberty and authority on which I wish to focus.

Much depends on how we define authority. We could approach the matter gently by translating the issue into one of limits. For, of course, we can speak of liberation from the limitations of slavery, or from the limitations of the prison cell. The obvious point then emerges at once, that there is no freedom to transcend natural and physical limitations: we are not free to be present physically in two places at the same time; we are not free to fly unaided like a bird; we are not free to live unaided below the surface of the sea; we are not free to increase our height or extend our life. But what about artificially imposed limits? Is the footballer free who carries on dribbling beyond the touch line? Is the musician free who ignores all the bar lines and time signatures? In such cases it can be argued that liberty can achieve its full flowering only when expressed within recognized and agreed limitations. This is at the heart of Newman's protest against liberalism's making claims beyond its competence. Yet it is precisely at such points that the tension re-emerges. For it was out of the refusal to accept such limitations that some of the greatest advances in human knowledge and skill have emerged: for example, the realization that the universe was heliocentric, the possibility of manned flight, new developments in the performing arts.

The issue is usually posed in terms of freedom from coercion – freedom from being forced to do what you do not want to do, or what is not in your own interests. The model of slavery or of the enslaved people once again springs to mind. But what about a free person or a free people? Can they be coerced into unwilling action or prevented by force of law from doing what they want? Yes of course, if their failure to act in the one case or their action in the other actually harms others. But what if it does not harm others? Can a free citizen be forced to vote or to fight in a war or to eat or refrain from eating certain foods? Then there are the questions which trouble us today: Is it right to legislate against homosexual acts in private between consenting adults? Is it right to compel free citizens to wear seat belts for their own protection? Is it right to treat the drug-taker as a criminal? It could be argued that coercion is permitted when it would prevent greater evils. But who then should decide what are these 'evils' and whether they are 'greater'? – a question to which we will return.

The most difficult of the formulations of the tension is that between liberty and authority as such. John Stuart Mill can describe the history of his theme simply as 'the struggle between liberty and authority'.[17] Though he is thinking mostly in terms of coercion, it is clear also that the authority from which such liberty seeks to be free can include the authority of state and church, of parents and elders. Where the liberty of the individual is paramount, authority by definition stands in question, its currency debased. In theology we naturally think of the whole movement of Liberal Protestantism, at whose heart was the fundamental questioning of the authority of tradition and the demand that all claims to truth be subject to inquiry

---

17 Mill, *Liberty* p. 59.

and test. Despite Newman's protest, such Liberalism cannot be dismissed simply as Christian faith succumbing to rationalism. For it encapsulated the lasting insight that all our knowledge is incomplete, all expressions of truth are fallible and corrigible. Any opinion or belief which is not open to scrutiny and argument is being held, Mill would justifiably claim, 'as a dead dogma, not a living truth'.[18] And yet, where does liberalism become license, when the old currency is not simply debased but replaced by license to print a wholly new currency? Where does legitimate questioning of traditional forms and formulae become a jettisoning of the whole?

Here not least it may be important to recognize *the experience of liberation as the critical moment of liberty.* For in that experience the tension between liberty and authority is maintained – precisely as an interaction with the authority, precisely as a dialogue with the tradition, even when its authority is being radically questioned. It is when such interaction and dialogue is abandoned that liberty becomes something else. It may be anarchy, or it may be a new dogmatism. But when it ceases to be in tension with that from which it has been liberated, then it is no longer liberty. This is precisely the danger of theological Liberalism. Precisely as an expression of freedom *from*, it is only viable and sustainable when it remains fully attached to its roots. When it ceases to be in living relationship with that in relation to which it proclaims itself as free, it loses the sustenance which comes from that root, the constant challenge which reinvigorates the vision of liberty and conditions its expression. Without the experience of liberation, liberty can become a mere cypher, and without the experience of liberty in tension with authority, liberalism offers no enduring hope.

---

18 Mill, *Liberty* p. 97.

Here too we see a consequence of the word 'liberal' losing its natural antithesis in 'servile' and becoming simply an alternative to 'conservative'. It is somewhat ironic that in the wake of the Enlightenment, as slavery itself became an increasingly pressing moral issue, so liberalism could claim the opposing positive moral high ground. Whereas when slavery ceased to be a major factor in Western society, liberalism lost its most apposite antithesis and could be given a much more negative connotation, and be made a whipping boy for those who wish to cling to and assert traditional values. Once again, then, it is important in posing the contrast between liberty and authority to recall that the essence of liberty is the experience of liberation from a merely servile acquiescence to authoritarian claims. The tension between liberty and authority is only partially grasped if it is limited to the tension between liberal and conservative. The heart of liberty remains the act of liberation from the status of slave.

4. Liberty and the self

So far we have discussed the concept of liberty primarily in terms of freedom *from*. What about freedom *to*? Liberty from is a negative quality, unless it is also liberty which has a positive purpose – liberty to be, to do, to achieve. The middle-aged among us will recall that this was one of the major failings of the student revolution in France in 1968. The leaders were clear enough on what they were rebelling against, but when asked what it was they wanted to put in place of the old structures they could offer no vision. To the question, 'Liberty for what?' they could offer no substantive or coherent answer. So too there are Christians whose whole concept of liberty is so focussed on that moment of conversion or subsequent experience of cleansing or renewal, that they have hardly begun to think in practical terms what they have been thus liberated for.

An old Greek saying expressed the answer in terms of self-choosing: 'The free man is one who lives as he chooses.'[19] But that will hardly do in itself, as the Greeks of course realized, since the inner passions could be more enslaving than any outward coercion. Similarly the more modern romantic idealization of nature as a state of liberty (the myth of 'the noble savage') begs the question as to what humankind's true nature is. It was precisely liberalism's too optimistic assumption that humanity was steadily evolving towards some more perfect moral society which was destroyed by the horrifying evidence of man's inhumanity to man in the carnage of the 1914–18 war and the unspeakable horror of the Holocaust, devastating blows from which theological liberalism has never recovered.

As the measure of liberty, the Greek ideals of self-sufficiency and self-knowledge had more to commend them. In Cynic and Stoic philosophy the self-sufficient man was one who was sufficient to himself (*autarkeia*), able to realize his own inner possibilities, independent and in need of no one else. And the ancient Greek proverb, 'Know thyself', remained an ideal throughout the Hellenistic period; knowledge liberates by eliminating the fears and desires which arise from ignorance or superstition. These remain valid and challenging ideals, but they have been undermined in one degree or other by the insights of psychology, and the increased awareness of the reality of deep conditioning of self-perception through inheritance and upbringing, and the possibility of self-deception. Luther had already

---

19 See e.g. *TDNT* 2.490.

provided a basis for a theological analysis along such lines by his shrewd perception of the degree to which a works-mentality can be self-deceptive in the assessment of what makes a person acceptable to God.

In the 19th century the measure of liberty became again the human mind; freedom is freedom to live as a rational being. Mill says quite openly that his 'doctrine is meant to apply only to human beings in the maturity of their faculties'.[20] By that he means to exclude children and minors. But it is clear that the range of exclusion must run further. For he limits the application of liberty 'to the time when mankind have become capable of being improved by free and equal discussion', to man as a 'moral being . . . capable of rectifying his mistakes by discussion and experience'.[21] This, in the words of Eliza Doolittle's father, is 'middle class morality'.[22] It has fallen into the intellectual's trap of assuming that what is clear to him must be equally persuasive to others – that is, in the event, to others like himself, able to sustain a 'free and equal discussion' with the likes of himself. But why should rational men be entitled to exercise their liberty in the satisfaction of their desired ends more than irrational men?

Moreover, are we to treat rationality as a new infallible voice of God, and irrationalism as a new heresy, the fallibility and sinfulness of which excludes the non-rational or less rational from the courts of liberty? Is reason or ratiocination a supreme good, a universal, unadulterated source of all truth into which we plug or in which we engage? Here too the problems of self-deception cannot be ignored. We need to recall, for example, the whole debate between determinism and libertarianism. Even if we do not hold to a

---

20 Mill, *Liberty* p. 69.
21 Mill, *Liberty* pp. 69, 80.
22 George Bernard Shaw, *Pygmalion* (1912) Act 11.

thoroughgoing determinist position, can we make sufficient allowance for the degree to which our rationality has been determined by forces over which we have no control, and whose beneficent character cannot be guaranteed? The free man may be ruled by his reason, but is his reason free? We need only recall the recent debates about the causes of the riots on Tyneside[23] to realize how complex such questions are. Were they the result of freely chosen wickedness, or of social conditioning? One would hardly want to dispense with categories of responsibility, of praise and blame. But if social deprivation is a significant factor in such occurrences, how free in the event, how free in the terms used by Mill were those guilty of rioting?

And what of the common experience of divided counsel within, when 'I am not myself', or when I find another law warring in my members, the thoughts awhile accusing, awhile excusing? Is the true self the rational self, or the instinctive self, the spirit or the mind, in Philo's terms, the higher soul or the lower soul? Socrates speaks of the blessings of madness (Plato, *Phaedrus* 244a–245a),[24] and the Jewish and Christian traditions give high priority to the experience of prophecy. For they both recognized that the mind left to itself alone could remain entrapped in the weaknesses of the human condition, and that without such experiences of inspiration humankind would remain immeasurably poorer, limited rather than liberated by their powers of rational thought.

In short, is the self, its satisfaction and self-esteem, the measure of human freedom or of its perversion? This brings us to our final line of reflection.

---

23 Riots particularly in the Meadowell district of Newcastle in the summer of 1991. The resulting debate included disagreement between local clergy and the Archbishop of Canterbury.

24 See particularly E. R. Dodds, *The Greeks and the Irrational* (Berkeley: University of California, 1951) p. 64.

5. Liberty and society

The other area of tension within the concept and practice of liberty lies on the interface between the individual and society. How are the demands and rights of the two to be reconciled? One answer in Greek thought was to extend the ideal of self-sufficiency, to retreat into an inner citadel as little touched by the world as possible, as free from the downward drag of the passions as possible. Then of course one could be free, with desire for worldly glory or sensual pleasure resisted and mastered. Such disengagement from too harsh reality and from society has been an ideal of considerable influence in Christian (and other) mystical and quietist traditions. But is it liberty? Such self-denial may be admirable, but is it an expression of freedom? To cut oneself off from anything and everything which might threaten or injure is to long for death. Is *that* the alternative to living within the tensions and competing demands of community?

In the modern period the concern rather has been to focus on the liberty of the individual in active relationship with and within society and to mark out clear limits between the state and the individual. As already indicated, the classic statement of individual liberty is that of John Stuart Mill. In a much quoted passage he reduces the issue to 'one very simple principle'.

> That principle is that the sole end for which mankind are warranted, individually or collectively, in interfering with the liberty of action of any of their number is self-protection. That the only purpose for which power can be rightfully exercised over any member of a civilized community, against his will, is to prevent harm to others. . . . The only part of the conduct of anyone for which he is amenable to society is that which concerns others. In the part which merely concerns

himself, his independence is, of right, absolute. Over himself, over his own body and mind, the individual is sovereign.[25]

And later he summarizes again: 'The only freedom which deserves the name is that of pursuing our own good in our own way, so long as we do not attempt to deprive others of theirs or impede their efforts to obtain it.'[26]

In all this Mill's hostility to society is clear. He is concerned about 'the tyranny of the majority', about 'social tyranny more formidable than many kinds of political oppression', about 'the tyranny of the prevailing opinion and feeling', about the intolerances of 'that miscellaneous collection of a few wise and many foolish individuals called the public'.[27] He thus identifies the temptations ever before the majority to coerce the minority, the enticing character of a rationale which claims to know best and can justify pressure to conform by the specious argument that if the victims were truly enlightened they would conform willingly.[28] In this protest of indomitable individualism there is much to be treasured.

He also makes an impassioned plea for diversity: that diversity is necessary if truth is to prosper and advance. Competition and collision of opinion are necessary, otherwise truth will degenerate into dead dogma. 'The Christian system is no exception to the rule that in an imperfect state of the human mind the interests of truth require a diversity of opinions'. Individual vigour and manifold diversity are what together produce originality. The plea even encom-

25 Mill, *Liberty* pp. 68–9.
26 Mill, *Liberty* p. 72.
27 Mill, *Liberty* pp. 2–3, 81.
28 This, of course, was the rationale of the Inquisition, and is well illustrated for the 20th century under Communism by Arthur Koestler's *Darkness at Noon* (1941).

passes a defence of eccentricity: 'Precisely because the tyranny of opinion is such as to make eccentricity a reproach, it is desirable, in order to break through that tyranny, that people should be eccentric.'[29] Here too is an insight worth preserving and maintaining.

The argument naturally includes a plea for toleration.

> If all mankind minus one were of one opinion, mankind would be no more justified in silencing that one person than he, if he had the power, would be justified in silencing mankind. . . . If the opinion is right, they are deprived of the opportunity of exchanging error for truth; if wrong, they lose, what is almost as great a benefit, the clearer perception and livelier impression of truth produced by its collision with error. . . . We can never be sure that the opinion we are endeavouring to stifle is a false opinion; and if we were sure, stifling it would be an evil still.[30]

Such sentiments should also be weighed and given full measure.

And yet in all this the over-exaltation of the individual and the constant interposition of distance between individual and society has something frightening about it. Mill recognizes, of course, that the individual has some responsibility within society, to maintain, for example, indispensable common services; and any exercise of individual liberty which harms others can properly be forbidden and restrained by the organs of society. But he does not seem to take sufficiently seriously that exercise of individual liberty can impinge on and restrict the freedom of others in a whole complex variety of ways and degrees; no man is an island. It is Mill's individualism which is at the heart of the *laissez-faire* economics of the late 19th century,

---

29 Mill, *Liberty* pp. 114, 132.
30 Mill, *Liberty* pp. 76–7.

whose infringement on the human liberties of many work people was only tardily recognized.

It is also Mill's passionate belief that men are made human by their capacity for choice, by freedom to choose whether good or evil. That runs strangely counter to the Jewish and Christian insight that it was man's free choice of evil which lies at the heart of human fallenness.[31] And what about humankind as made in the image of a God who freely creates and gives graciously? Is it the individual's freedom to choose or freedom to love the other which constitutes his or her true humanity? Such issues have resurfaced in the last decade or so with the re-emergence of Mill's individualistic liberal ethic as the basis of Government policy idealizing once again the free market. Does the liberty of some to exercise choice in education and health actually reduce the liberty of the rest to enjoy an education and health service more adequately funded? Has the liberty Mill pleads for ever been demanded by any but a small minority of highly educated and self-conscious people? Despite Mill's own abhorrence of social tyranny, is his not the voice of a privileged elite pressurizing others against their own interests, and does he see no danger of a tyranny of the well-educated? 'Paternalism', says Kant, 'is the greatest despotism imaginable.'[32]

One other point perhaps worth making is that in the modern world the real test of liberty is not so much the liberty of the individual but the liberty of minority societies – the Kurds in Iraq, the Christians in southern Sudan, the Tamils in Sri Lanka, the Catholics in

---

31 This was a point I attempted to make in an open letter to Mrs Thatcher in response to her 'sermon on the Mound' to the General Assembly of the Church of Scotland ('Faith to Faith: A Theology of Freedom at Other People's Expense', The *Guardian*, May 30, 1988, p. 3).
32 Cited by Berlin p. 137.

Northern Ireland, the Indians in Brazil, and so on. The break up of eastern Europe has posed the issue in its sharpest form in the second half of the 20th century for a continent grown smug and complacent over the supposed maturity of its political systems. Nor has the problem of ethnic minorities yet been fully addressed in our own society. What is at stake here is not simply the rights of individuals, but communal values which are diverse, religious and cultural traditions and customs which are in conflict with those of the majority. The liberty of individualism has an insufficient answer here, precisely because the liberty requested is not the liberty of individuals but the liberty of communities. There is no alternative here but to seek to create and develop a free society, where there are both common values, genuine reverence for the traditions and institutions of society which have grown over the years to protect liberty, and a full blooded and generous recognition of and tolerance for the diversities which are integral to the identity of the different groups who make up the society.

To round off this point a passage from F. A. Hayek provides a fitting conclusion.

> Coercion may sometimes be avoidable only because a high degree of voluntary conformity exists, which means that voluntary conformity may be a condition of a beneficial working of freedom. It is indeed a truth, which all the great apostles of freedom outside the rationalistic school have never tired of emphasizing, that freedom has never worked without deeply ingrained moral beliefs and that coercion can be reduced to a minimum only where individuals can be expected as a rule to conform voluntarily to certain principles.[33]

---

33 Hayek p. 62. He quotes Burke: 'Men are qualified for civil liberty, in exact proportion to their disposition to put moral chains upon their appetites; in proportion as their love of justice is above their rapacity; in

6. Conclusions

Here then are three themes worthy of further consideration under the heading of Christian liberty – liberty and authority, liberty and the self, liberty and society or community. And these are the three subjects of the following lectures. As already indicated I cannot hope to do these themes anything like sufficient justice. As a student of the New Testament and Christian beginnings I must limit my more detailed analyses to the areas of my own specialism.

On the other hand I see no need to apologize for treating such a large subject on this more limited front. For Jesus and Christian beginnings provide a sequence of remarkably appropriate test cases on just the topics indicated. Christianity, after all, began as a movement within a larger, more established framework of order and tradition, began, indeed, precisely by questioning older, established authority; and at an early stage in its own development it could not help but address questions of personal freedom for individuals and in relation to society. We may even describe Christianity in its initial emergence as a kind of liberation movement; among its first spokesmen Paul is not alone in using the image of the exodus to illuminate the significance of Christian beginnings. And the New Testament as a whole can certainly be described as the charter of Christian liberty, more fundamental than any of the great Declarations of Human Rights and liberties of later centuries. However wide the resources needed

---

proportion as their soundness and sobriety of understanding is above their vanity and presumption; in proportion as they are more disposed to listen to the council of the wise and good, in preference to the flattery of knaves'; and Tocqueville: 'Liberty cannot be established without morality, nor morality without faith' (Hayek pp. 435–6 n. 36).

to define liberty, the definition of Christian liberty is given in the New Testament as nowhere else.

In the second lecture, therefore, we will turn without further apology to our series of test cases drawn from the earliest years of Christianity, starting with Jesus and authority.

CHAPTER TWO

Jesus and Authority

1. Introduction

The first test case which invites exploration is naturally
Jesus himself. What does Jesus have to say to us on the
subject of Christian liberty? As the founding or central
figure in Christianity does he somehow epitomize
Christian liberty?

An immediate problem is that Jesus himself appar-
ently said very little on the theme of liberty. The noun
'freedom' occurs nowhere in the Gospels. Matthew's
Gospel contains the one enigmatic reference, 'Then the
sons are free' (Matt. 17:26), to which we will have to
return. John's Gospel has that single complex in 8:32–
36, 'You will know the truth and the truth will make
you free', and so on, to which we referred in the
previous lecture. But the question of whether John's
Gospel preserves a historical record or an elaborated
meditation is particularly serious at this point, given
not least that the context contains, on the one hand,
one of the most virulent pieces of anti-Jewish polemic
in the NT (8:44), and on the other, one of the highest
expressions of christology in the NT (8:58).[1] Otherwise

---

1 See e.g. my *The Partings of the Ways between Christianity and Judaism*
(London: SCM/Philadelphia: TPI, 1991) chaps. 8 and 11.

there is total silence. Apart from these two problematic passages we have nothing in the Gospels which bears so explicitly on the theme of freedom.[2]

At the same time, however, the relevance of Jesus to our topic is hardly to be determined simply by a word count of 'freedom' words in the Gospels. For a large part of the fascination which Jesus exerts on students of history is the significance of the man himself. I do not mean here his significance for Christian faith as such, questions of incarnation, atonement and such like. These are further and important topics. But even limiting ourselves to a less overtly confessional approach, the significance of Jesus can hardly be denied. For Jesus is a fulcrum figure, a pivotal figure, one on whom history turned, the history of great movements, the history of whole epochs. He appears in history as a Jew, one 'born under the law', 'a servant of the circumcised', as Paul puts it (Gal. 4:4; Rom. 15:8); and from him emerges a quite different religion – Christianity. He appears as one who belonged to one system of religion, and from him stemmed a whole new system of religion. Such a transition has obvious parallels with the situations which we have seen in the previous lecture to epitomize liberty – the movement from an old order to a new, experienced as liberation – the transition from minority to majority, experienced as a setting free into adulthood.

This suggests that Jesus provides us a test case for the first area briefly explored in the previous lecture – Liberty and Authority. Was Jesus perhaps a Diogenes-like figure, whose life of protest spoke louder than his words? Was he like a Luther, who set his face

---

2 We should also note two Lukan passages. In Luke 4:18 *aphesis*, which usually means 'pardon, forgiveness', is used in the sense 'release' (following the LXX of Isa. 61:1). And in Luke 13:12, 16 *(apo)luo* is used in the sense 'to release' from the bondage (by Satan) of a crippling condition.

deliberately against the authority of the old order, or like a Gorbachev, who became a catalyst, setting in train a course of events which ran far beyond what he could ever have imagined? What does Jesus say to us, by word or deed, on the theme of liberty and authority?

2. Who or what were the authorities in Jesus' time?

We must begin by clarifying what constituted the authority in relation to which Jesus might be said to have called for or exercised freedom. The picture is reasonably clear, but care must be taken lest we draw it in exaggerated outline.[3]

a) In the first place there was what we can call the *secular* authority; 'civil authority' we should probably avoid, since in a state which functioned as a temple state, with a religious constitution, civil and religious authority were inextricably intertwined. By secular authority we mean above all the power of the Roman Empire – Judea and Galilee being, in modern terms, occupied territories. This authority would be there in the background throughout Jesus' life and ministry, particularly with memories of the last Jewish revolt organized by Judas 'the Galilean', albeit in Judea (AD 6), still fresh, and the knowledge that their taxes (poll tax and land tax) no doubt went towards the tribute which Herod paid to Rome. But otherwise the day by day impact of Roman authority in rural Galilee would have been small.

Moreover, since Galilee was part of the territory of Herod Antipas, his administration would constitute the more immediate secular authority in Galilee. So too any

---

3 E. Schürer, *The History of the Jewish People in the Age of Jesus Christ*, revised and edited G. Vermes et al. (Edinburgh: T. & T. Clark; 4 volumes, 1973–87) continues to provide the best and most detailed overview.

military personnel with whom Jesus came in contact would likely be members of Herod's Jewish forces rather than Italian soldiers or Roman auxiliaries. Likewise taxes, both direct and indirect (custom duties, tolls and tariffs), would be levied in the name of Herod, with the latter leased out to *publicani*, tax-collectors. Since the burden of taxation was notably oppressive, the pressures of taxation and consequent unpopularity of the tax-collectors would be a factor of daily life.[4]

Judea and Jerusalem, on the other hand were under the direct rule of Roman prefects, like Pontius Pilate, and Roman administrative and military authority would have been much more in evidence there, especially during the main Jewish festivals, when the Prefect moved from Caesarea to Jerusalem in order to be on hand with sufficient forces in case of trouble. The Roman garrison in the Antonia fortress, the not infrequent exercise of capital punishment, the Roman right to appoint the High Priest, and several blundering attempts by Pilate to demonstrate his authority (carrying ensigns bearing the image of the emperor into Jerusalem, appropriating funds from the Temple treasury to build an aqueduct, the slaughter of some Galileans about to present their offerings in Jerusalem) would all provide regular reminders of the power of Roman authority over the lives of all Judeans.

b) The more direct power, however, was exercised by *religious* authority, above all the Sanhedrin, to whom the Romans entrusted the direction of the nation and a wide range of legislative and executive responsibilities. That meant especially the high-priestly aristocracy, supported by distinguished laymen, who main-

---

4 In both cases the historical evidence needs to be more closely consulted if misleading pictures of the context of Jesus' mission are to be avoided and inappropriate corollaries drawn out in text-book and sermon. See now E. P. Sanders, *Judaism. Practice and Belief 63 BCE–66CE* (London: SCM/Philadelphia: TPI, 1992) chap. 9.

tained leadership of the Sanhedrin throughout this period, with the High Priest always as its president. That Pharisaic views had some hold within the ranks of the Sanhedrin, so that some members could indeed be called Pharisees, does not change the fact that the power of the Sanhedrin was invested primarily in the aristocratic Sadducean, that is, priestly faction.[5]

The authority of the high priesthood was also a natural consequence of the significance of the Temple in Jewish life.[6] Judea was a temple state: it existed as a recognizable entity only in order to service the Jerusalem Temple. As a viable economic unit Judea depended entirely on the Temple – the flow of Temple tax revenues from all over the diaspora amounting to a massive sum, the constant stream of sacrifices and pilgrims with all the supporting trade and industry, the huge influx of the three great pilgrim festivals in particular, not to mention the huge rebuilding pro-gramme which continued throughout this period, in-evitably involving large numbers of tradesmen, craftsmen and artists – all these gave the Temple authorities who controlled these resources an un-paralleled power within Judea. And above all, of course, the Temple had all the power of a national cult centre, the religious symbol which captured the hearts of all Israelites as nothing else could, the place where God had chosen to put his name, holy Zion, the point of effective contact between heaven and earth. The Temple was a focus of religious authority *par excellence*.

c) In listing the sources of authority in the Palestine of Jesus' time a pre-eminent place must also be given to the *Torah*, the Law in particular, or, more generally,

---

5 Note again important qualifications indicated by Sanders, *Judaism* pp. 472–90.

6 See e.g. my *Partings* pp. 31–5.

the Law and the Prophets (and Writings). The Law was
also the law of the land, not only religious but also civil
law. It was the one text-book in the education of Jewish
youth. It provided the framework for life and all
relationships. Above all it was the word of God, the
instruction given by God to direct the lives of his
people. Its authority was therefore all pervasive in the
life of any Jew, even the only nominally devout.

Its authority would come to bear in particular
instances in different ways. One would be, of course,
through the knowledge of it given in and retained from
earlier education (boys only). Another would be
through the constant reminder of the content of the
Law in readings and expositions in the meeting houses
on Galilean sabbaths, though whether we can yet speak
of 'synagogues' and complete 'synagogue services' is a
matter of debate.[7] Another would be through rulings
on disputed points provided by local priests, but now
increasingly by lay experts, scribes, the *sopherim*, or
Torah scholars, described in our Gospels also as
'lawyers' or 'teachers of the law' (e.g. Matt. 22:35;
Luke 5:17; 7:30).[8]

It is here that we can begin to speak of the Pharisees
proper. As a body they included many scribes. What
marked them out, particularly over against the Saddu-
cees, was their recognition that a law drawn up many
centuries earlier inevitably required elaboration and
interpretation to demonstrate its continuing authority
over different and unforeseen circumstances. This is
usually described as the 'oral law', but would not be
regarded as something different from the Torah by the
Pharisees, simply application of the Law itself. In

---

7 See discussion in S. J. D. Cohen, *From Maccabees to the Mishnah*
(Philadelphia: Westminster, 1987) pp. 111–5; also H. C. Kee, 'The
Transformation of the Synagogue after 70 CE: its Import for Early
Christianity', *New Testament Studies* 36 (1990) pp. 1–24.
8 See again Sanders, *Judaism* pp. 170–82.

developing this *Halakah*, rulings on how one should 'walk' in accordance with the Law,[9] their concern was not only to apply the Law more accurately, as Josephus tells us,[10] but also to ameliorate its demands where necessary to make it possible to live fully within the Law thus understood.

Since the Pharisees have had such 'bad press' in Christian tradition, I should simply add two comments, now fortunately being stressed in recent scholarship. First, Pharisees were not the dominant authority at this time, but only one faction within second Temple Judaism claiming a fuller insight into and practice of the Law.[11] Although they were a growing influence, it would be quite inaccurate to describe them as the representatives of 'Judaism' as such, as though there was only one Judaism at this time, or as though there was already an agreed concept of 'normative or orthodox Judaism'. A Jew could disagree with Pharisees without ceasing to be a Jew, or indeed, without ceasing to be a Pharisee with a different halakah. Second, within the spectrum of second Temple Judaism, the Pharisees were relatively *liberal* in their rulings. In contrast, the Sadducaic refusal to move beyond the written Torah as such was markedly conservative, and the Essene rulings were decidedly more rigorous.[12]

---

9 The term 'Halakah' is derived from the Hebrew *halak* meaning 'to walk'.

10 Josephus, *Jewish War* 1.108–9; 2.162; *Life* 191; *Jewish Antiquities* 20.200–1; also Acts 22.3 and 26.5.

11 At the time of Herod they were only 6,000 in number, according to Josephus, *Antiquities* 13.298; 18.20; 17.42.

12 Cf. e.g. the evidence of the Dead Sea scroll fragments known as 4QMMT, as described by L. H. Schiffman, 'The Temple Scroll and the Systems of Jewish Law of the Second Temple Period', *Temple Scroll Studies*, ed. G. J. Brooke (Sheffield: Sheffield Academic, 1989) pp. 245–51. It has only recently been published – by R. Eisenman & M. Wise, *The Dead Sea Scrolls Uncovered* (Shaftesbury, Dorset: Element, 1992) pp. 182–96.

d) Finally we should note the authority of *social convention*, recalling what Mill referred to as 'social tyranny', 'the tyranny of the prevailing opinion and feeling, . . . the tendency of society to impose, by other means than civil penalties, its own ideas and practices as rules of conduct on those who dissent from them'.[13] At this distance in time we have little prospect of building up a clear, let alone full picture of such pressures in the Palestine of Jesus' day. But three instances come at once to mind, though the line between law and convention is, as always in such cases, rather fine.

One example has already been hinted at – the social antipathy to taxcollectors, judged no doubt by the mass of their fellows who suffered under their administration to have betrayed their community's trust and lost any claim to their community's respect. Since excessive taxation was destroying the livelihoods of not a few at this time and driving some to banditry, the social antagonism against taxcollectors must often have been intense. Here we may mention also those linked with taxcollectors in our Gospels – sinners; that is, those judged by others who thought of themselves as 'righteous' to have set themselves against the law by their life-style.[14]

A second example is the strength of antipathy towards foreigners, a common feature in one degree or other of all societies. This was also a reflection of Israel's sense of election and of the holiness of Zion and of the land of Israel: the foreigner was literally 'lawless', outside the law, outlaws; Gentiles were by definition 'sinners'; if Israel was holy, beyond Israel's

---

13 *Liberty* p. 63.
14 See my 'Pharisees, Sinners and Jesus', *Jesus, Paul and the Law. Studies in Mark and Galatians* (London: SPCK/Louisville: Westminster, 1990) pp. 71–7.

borders lay only impurity.[15] Hostility was particularly strong against the Samaritans, regarded as a bastard race with an apostate religion[16] – typical of the hostility which in the history of nations and peoples has always been directed against the close neighbour whose very proximity most threatens 'our' boundary and identity.

The third segment of society who suffered from the authority of social convention and prejudice was women. As illustration, I need only remind you of the clearly drawn purity rules which meant that during her normal child-bearing years a woman would be ritually impure for at least a quarter of every month (Lev. 15). The primary consequence was exclusion from the Temple during these periods; but it would also be socially crippling in a society where ritual purity outside the Temple was taken seriously. The point is symbolized in the structure of the Temple itself, with the court of women *outside* the court of Israel. In more general terms a woman was set under the authority of her father and on marriage passed under the authority of her husband. And only the husband had full rights to sue for divorce; in Jewish law and custom there was no question of the woman having equal rights to divorce her husband.[17]

This all too brief survey of secular and religious authority, of the authority of Torah and of social convention in the Palestine of Jesus' time will have to suffice for present purposes. If Jesus is to serve as a test

---

15 See for example my *Partings* pp. 38–42. Jewish hostility to foreigners, however, can be greatly exaggerated. We should note, e.g., the traditional concern shown for the resident alien and the welcome given to proselyte and God-fearing Gentile in many diaspora synagogues (some details are available in my *Jesus, Paul and the Law* pp. 142–7).

16 For fuller details see e.g. J. D. Purvis, 'The Samaritans and Judaism', *Early Judaism and its Modern Interpreters*, ed. R. A. Kraft & G. W. E. Nickelsburg (Atlanta: Scholars, 1986) chap. 3.

17 See e.g. B. Witherington, *Women in the Ministry of Jesus* (Cambridge: Cambridge University, 1984) pp. 2–6.

case for the issue of liberty and authority it is in these areas we will have to look.

3. Jesus and secular authority

I do not intend here to open up again the old question of whether Jesus should be regarded as a political revolutionary, an heir of Judas the Galilean and forerunner of the Zealots. There is simply insufficient evidence to sustain such a thesis, despite the local advocacy of S. G. F. Brandon.[18] For example, the choice of Simon the 'zealot' as one of the twelve is relevant only if 'zealot' was already an established nickname for a freedom fighter, and that is far from clear; Paul was a 'zealot' (Gal. 1:14), but not against the Romans. And the report of revolutionary fervour among the crowd after the episode known as the feeding of the five thousand, the attempt to take Jesus by force and make him king (according to John 6:15), concludes with the clear indication that Jesus wanted nothing to do with such an attempt or aspiration (cf. Mark 6:45ff).

The hypothesis that Jesus advocated violent rebellion is particularly vulnerable at two points. For one thing it has to hypothesize an almost total whitewash of the Jesus tradition to remove all (or almost all) of the tell-tale signs.[19] But any thesis which has to read the great bulk of its argument into (rather than out of) the text is out of control and beyond serious debate; as J. B. Lightfoot comments on another front, 'In the land of

---

18 Particularly his *Jesus and the Zealots* (Manchester: Manchester University, 1967; but see E. Bammel & C. F. D. Moule, eds., *Jesus and the Politics of his Day* (Cambridge: Cambridge University, 1984).
19 The strongest of such left-over elements would be Luke 22:35–38.

the unverifiable there are no efficient critical police.'[20] Secondly, it is scarcely credible that Jesus should have advocated violent revolution, or that he should have made a serious military attempt to seize the Temple mount (now concealed behind the whitewash of the 'cleansing of the Temple'), without provoking prompt military response from the Roman authorities. Pilate made short shrift of such potential trouble in Samaria a few years later, and the garrison of the Antonia fortress, strengthened as usual for the Passover feast, and overlooking the Temple platform precisely to ensure control there, would have been quick to nip in the bud any serious threat to public order in the court of the Temple, as Acts later attests in the case of Paul (Acts 21:31–36).

The picture we gain from the Gospels is a rather more 'quietistic' one – Jesus working within the constraints of the political system, rather than overtly against them. It is perhaps significant that he is never recalled as entering the two main political and administrative centres in Galilee – Sepphoris (just over the hill from Nazareth) and Tiberias – suggesting perhaps a wish to avoid potentially inflammatory controversy (since many Jews reared on the heroic tales of the Maccabean resistance to Hellenization two centuries earlier would no doubt have regarded them as foreign impositions and institutions antipathetic to the theological integrity and traditions of the Jewish people). Unlike John the Baptist, Jesus is not recalled as saying anything which would have been taken as a direct personal attack on the ruling family. Of two possible exceptions one is the warning in Mark 8:15, to 'beware of the leaven . . . of Herod', which comes in a section

---

20 J. B. Lightfoot, *Essays on Supernatural religion* (London: Macmillan, 1889) p. 36.

bearing by common consent the clearest indications of Markan composition in all the Gospel.[21] The other is Luke's report that Jesus called Herod Antipas 'that fox', that 'crafty one' (Luke 13:32); but the epithet is not particularly strong or offensive. The opposition of Herod which, according to Luke, brought that response from Jesus (Luke 13:31), and of the Herodians, at least according to Mark 3:6, does not seem to have been occasioned by any overtly political word or action on the part of Jesus.

In contrast, Jesus is shown as tolerant of the military: he sets before those compelled to offer assistance for one mile the example of someone who readily goes a second mile (Matt. 5:41); and he responds willingly to the plea for help from the centurion, whether a Gentile or a Jew in service of Herod (Matt. 8:5–13; John 4:46–54). More striking still, in the famous trick question about paying taxes to Caesar, his masterly response could hardly be interpreted as denying the right of Caesar to levy taxes, since he indicates that Caesar has a rightful sphere of authority, that there are 'things which are Caesar's' (Mark 12:14–17). Perhaps above all, the call to 'love your enemy', so distinctively Christian and almost certainly derived from Jesus, can hardly have been so cherished in Christian circles had it been known that Jesus advocated a quite other and more violent response to the Roman occupier. The fact seems to be that Jesus marched by a different drumbeat, owning primary allegiance to a different kingship, the kingship of God; and that enabled him to be relatively indifferent to the claims of other kings, unthreatened by them, finding it unnecessary to challenge them or to resist

---

21 See e.g. R. A. Guelich, *Mark* (Word Biblical Commentary, 34A; Dallas: Word, 1989) pp. 418–9.

their demands – a freedom even under the supreme secular authority.[22]

And yet the fact remains that Jesus was executed as a messianic pretender (Mark 15:26), in the context of allusion to an insurrection (Mark 15:7), and with the charge pressed that he did, after all, forbid tribute to Caesar (at least, according to Luke 23:2). It must be the case, therefore, that, despite his quietism, Jesus could be presented as a sufficiently serious threat to good order that execution was appropriate. By saying this I do not mean to ignore or underestimate the casual brutality with which executions of non-Roman citizens were often ordered and carried out within the Roman Empire. I mean simply to indicate that there must have been something about Jesus sufficiently disturbing and challenging to the secular authority for his execution to be seen as a desirable act, however plausible or implausible, legal or illegal it might be. If it was not a forthright appeal for freedom from abuses of power by the secular authority, then what was it? Here we must turn to our second area of inquiry.

4. Jesus and religious authority

It is a striking fact that the Synoptic Gospels never portray Jesus at odds with the power of the Sanhedrin, of the high priesthood and of the Temple until the very last week of his ministry. Even during that week Mark tells us that he was in the Temple day after day teaching without causing trouble (Mark 14:49). Earlier on, the most immediately relevant traditions indicate that he respected the authority of the priest to pro-

---

22 To the degree that they were no longer a major political force (as they had been earlier in their history) the same was true of the Pharisees at the time of Jesus.

nounce a leper clean (Mark 1:44; Luke 17:14), and
that he took for granted the continued operation of the
Temple cult in the offering of gifts on the altar (Matt.
5:23–24; Mark 1:44). To be sure, John puts the
'cleansing of the Temple' at the beginning of his Gospel
(2:13–20), but he also shows Jesus still going up to
Jerusalem for the feasts thereafter (5:1; 7:10). There is
not much striking free from the authority of the old
order here.

It could be argued, and I so argue elsewhere,[23] that
Jesus in effect undermined the authority of the Temple
by disregarding the purity legislation which had the
preservation of the sanctity of the Temple at its heart.
For example, he touches the leper, and responds
positively and without embarrassment to the plea of the
woman with the haemorrhage who touched him in the
crowd (Mark 1:40–45; 5:24–34). Similarly it could be
argued that his pronouncement of sins forgiven, without any reference whatsoever to the prerogative of the
priest to pronounce sins forgiven after presenting the
sin-offering in the Temple (Mark 2:5; Luke 7:48), was
in effect to undermine the authority of Temple and cult.
But if so, it was done without fanfare, and was
evidently not seen as an overt challenge to the religious
authorities. Charges to that effect certainly do not
feature in any record that we have of Jesus' trial.

The other passage of major interest is the one
already referred to – the only passage in the Synoptic
Gospels where Jesus says anything about freedom,
Matt. 17:24–26:

> When they came to Capernaum, the collectors of the
> Temple-tax came to Peter and said, 'Does not your
> teacher pay the Temple tax?' He said, 'Yes'. And when
> he came home, Jesus spoke to him first, saying, 'What

---

23 *Partings* pp. 42–6.

do you think, Simon? From whom do the kings of the earth collect toll or tribute? From their sons, or from others?' When he replied, 'From others', Jesus said to him, Then the sons are free.'

The passage is difficult, particularly when we include the next verse, where Jesus tells Peter to go and catch a fish and to pay the tax with the coin which he finds in its mouth (Matt. 17:27). But if the central dialogue does indeed go back to Jesus, at least in essence, then the point is reasonably clear:[24] those who stand in the more immediate relation of family to a ruler, either as his own children or as his own citizens, are exempt from taxes which those more distant from the ruler (citizens or foreigners) should expect to pay. The application in the case in point is also fairly clear: the sons must be those whose more immediate relationship with God meant that they were less dependent on the Temple to maintain that relationship; they were free in relation to the cult, because of their direct relation to God as his sons. In the context of Jesus' teaching and mission this presumably included Jesus' own disciples, whom he taught to address God with the intimate family mode of address as 'Father'. At the same time we are not encouraged to make allegorical identification of the 'others'.

Here at least then, we see Jesus sitting loose to the Temple cult, although if the content of the final verse is included, he was willing to continue supporting this central pillar of religious authority 'to avoid causing offence'. At all events, we have attested within the Synoptic tradition an assertion of freedom on the part of Jesus in relation to the main embodiment of religious authority of his day. It is not a strident assertion, not making it a point of principle for action, not ramming

---

24 See particularly U. Luz, *Das Evangelium nach Matthäus* (Evangelisch-Katholischer Kommentar; Zürich: Benziger; vol. 2, 1990) pp. 528–34.

it down others' throats. On the contrary, it is an assertion of consideration and tolerance as well as of privilege. But it is an assertion of freedom nevertheless, an assertion of spiritual independence from cult and religious hierarchy, and one potentially destructive of almost any religious structure, Quakers apart.

The only other evidence to be considered is the 'cleansing of the Temple' (Mark 11:15–17) and the accusation at his trial that Jesus had said something about destroying the Temple and rebuilding it again (Mark 14:58). The discussion of what Jesus actually did and said still remains as lively as ever.[25] It must suffice to note here that neither can be seen simply as a criticism or condemnation of the Temple and cult as such. It was doubtless a criticism of the present ordering of the cult; of abuses of the system by its guardians, the high priestly faction, quite likely; Mark's talk of 'a den of robbers' (echoing Jer. 7:11), and his setting the episode within the cursing of the barren fig tree certainly point in that direction.

But in Mark Jesus also envisages the Temple functioning as 'a house of prayer for all the nations' (Mark 11:17); and the saying about the destruction of the Temple includes talk of its rebuilding, in John 2:19, where it appears on Jesus' own lips, as well as in the false accusation in the Markan trial. In short, we can speak about an act of rebellion against the cult as it then operated, a further affirmation of freedom over against the most majestic symbol of religious authority of the time, but not in this case an assertion of freedom from Temple and cult as such.

We should simply add that it was almost certainly because of Jesus' action and teaching in reference to the Temple that decisive action was finally taken against him. It was because he was thus perceived as a threat to

---

25 See e.g. my *Partings* pp. 47–51.

religious authority, and evidently as a serious threat, that he was denounced and handed over to the secular authority to be executed on terms which the latter could accept. Whatever the loyalty he continued to express towards the Temple and its future role, however much he counselled continuing participation in and support for the Temple cult, his readiness to criticize it and (according to Matt. 17) to affirm the freedom of the sons of God in relation to it was evidently sufficient to seal his fate in the eyes of the religious authorities. As many of the prophets before (and after) him also found, those who speak on behalf of the liberty of the children of God will always be perceived as a threat to whatever religious hierarchy currently holds sway.

If then we can speak of Jesus expressing some degree of freedom in relation to the Temple and cult, what about his attitude to the other great institutional pillar of Jewish identity, both as a people and as a religion – the Law?

5. Jesus and the Torah

Like any educated Jewish youth, Jesus too would have been trained in Torah, he would have been a *bar mitzwah*, 'a son of the commandment'. The Law, in other words, provided precisely the sort of authority structure which a young man of independent thought might wish to question, precisely the sort of framework which someone seeking freedom from the old order might find it necessary to protest against. What do we find with Jesus? The subject is again much disputed, but a growing consensus in current scholarship finds itself more persuaded by the view that Jesus remained within the framework of the law and its authority. The *authority* with which he spoke was remarked on with surprise (Mark 1:27; 6:2; 11:28), presumably because he lacked any formal training, but the *content* of his teaching seems to have remained within the range of halakic discussion then possible within late second Temple Judaism.[26]

Thus we find him throughout his ministry in a positive relation with the synagogue or meeting house (Nazareth apart) – attending the synagogue 'as his custom was' according to Luke (4:16), accepting invitations to teach there (Matt. 9:35; Mark 1:21, 39; 6:2; Luke 13:10), and well disposed to synagogue rulers (Mark 5:22–43; but Luke 13:14). We cannot conclude from the evidence which we have that Jesus' wider teaching ministry, in the open, outside the synagogue, constituted a breach with the synagogue, the communal meeting place of the Galilean towns and villages.

So too it is significant that he himself is regularly called 'Teacher' (Mark 4:38; 5:35; 9:17, 38; 10:17, 20, 35; 12:14, 19, 32; 13:1; 14:14) – that is, teacher of Torah, for there was no other text-book in the curriculum, and one who radically divorced himself from the Torah would not have been called 'teacher', by interested audience and hostile Pharisee and Sadducee, as well as by his own disciples. So we are not surprised to hear of Jesus referring people to the law as something to be obeyed (as in Mark 1:44; 10:19), or being consulted on points of halakah (Mark 10:2; Luke 12:13), or appealing to the Torah as authority for his own teaching (Mark 12:26, 29–31). All this is quite apart from the more disputed passage in Matt. 5:17–20, where Jesus denies any intent to abolish anything in the law.

What does become apparent, however, is the radicalness of his teaching, what we might call *his*

---

26 See my *Partings* chap. 6.

readiness to appeal to first principles and to draw conclusions directly from them even when his conclusions ran counter to other parts of Torah. I am thinking here, for example, of his teaching on divorce, where by appeal to the fundamental principle of marriage enunciated in Gen. 2:24, he shows himself ready to disregard the Mosaic permission of divorce (Mark 10:2–9). Again, in Mark 7, he appeals to the primary responsibility of children to parents laid down in the decalogue and rebukes any suggestion that an offering vowed to the Temple might take higher precedence (7:9–13). Likewise, his more searching redefinition of the murder and adultery commandments (Matt. 5:21–22, 27–28), his subordination of the law of an eye for an eye and a tooth for a tooth to the love command (Matt. 5:38–48), his relative disparagement of the laws of clean and unclean in favour of inward purity (Mark 7:14–23), are all, in effect, calls for the Law to be written in the heart and for something far deeper than merely formal obedience.[27]

In short, we can speak of the freedom of Jesus in relation to the Torah. But it is not so much a freedom *from* the Torah, as a freedom *within* the Torah. Certainly there is no indication of an anxious concern for scrupulous observance in detail, or of a belief that the Torah is totally homogeneous or that all laws are of equal authority. Rather, there is a clear sense of freedom in the assessing and assertion of priorities where conflict arises. As his answer to the question about the greatest commandment underlines, the quality of relationship with God and the quality of interpersonal relationships always has the priority over any kind of merely mechanical obedience. In other

---

27 That this was a thoroughly Jewish (or OT) attitude to the law is demonstrated by such texts as Deut. 10:16; Jer. 4:4; 9:25–26; Ezek. 44:9; 1QpHab 11:13; 1QS 5:5; 1QH 2:18; 18:20.

circumstances and other ages such an attitude towards scripture would have been called 'liberal', expressing a freedom in the interpretation of scripture within the context of continuing respect for the authority of scripture, a setting out of priorities in such a way that when, for example, the first Christians abandoned the food laws they could appeal to the precedent set by Jesus (Mark 7:19).

The same point emerges in Jesus' disputes with that faction which otherwise was closest to Jesus in their attitude to the Torah – the Pharisees. I have already indicated that modern scholarship has drawn a much more sympathetic picture of the Pharisees than has traditionally obtained. But even so Jesus is remembered as having come into conflict with a number of Pharisees on a number of occasions. I have time here to mention only the most prominent conflict – regarding observance of the Sabbath – recalled in the two episodes in Mark of plucking ears of corn on the Sabbath and healing the withered hand of a man on the Sabbath (2:23–3:5).

What emerges here is precisely the same point. The dispute is not on *whether* the Sabbath should be observed, but on *how* it should be observed. Jesus is depicted not as calling for the abandonment of Sabbath observance, but as indicating what the attitude inculcated by the Sabbath should mean in practice. The Essene (we know for certain – CD 10–11) and Pharisee (presumably – as the Markan episodes imply) sought to safeguard the Sabbath by filling out the basic rule against working on the Sabbath in a multiplicity of case-laws, which they then sought to apply and enforce in their own circles. Jesus, in contrast, on both occasions, pressed behind the basic rule to the purpose of the Sabbath: it was given for the service of humankind, not for humankind to serve it (Mark 2:27); to do good and to save life can never be unlawful (Mark 3:4). That is to say, we have further examples of Jesus being willing to ignore what appears to be the obvious outworking of a particular law, and interpreting it in the light of the more fundamental demands of relationship with God and mutual relationships with others.

Here again, then, we have an example of radical freedom, because it was freedom within the Law, a freedom which could in due course be understood, in the different context of the Gentile mission, as a freedom from observance of that particular law altogether. It need hardly be added that those who in later centuries attempted to make Jesus' attitude towards the Sabbath into a new law, and to use that law to enforce a strict sabbatarianism,[28] have totally misunderstood the spirit of what Jesus did and said on the subject and the freedom it expressed.

Given then the evidence that Jesus lived out a significant degree of freedom in relation to both secular and religious authority, and not least in relation to the Torah, what of the final area of our inquiry – the more pervasive, but less quantifiable authority of social convention?

6. Jesus and social convention

Here the pattern which we have seen beginning to emerge is further confirmed and strengthened. This is evident in the three cases cited earlier to illustrate the power of social convention in the Palestinian society of Jesus' day.

I need hardly remind you, in the first place, that Jesus was notorious (I choose the word with care) for his association with taxcollectors and sinners (particu-

---

28 Such as we still find among the more conservative Presbyterian groupings in my native Scotland.

larly Mark 2:16–17; Matt. 11:19/Luke 7:39). Both
terms, as we have already noted, indicate those
regarded as unacceptable in a law-abiding, religious
community. By accepting commission to act as agents
for the secular power, with all the excessive demands
and swindles involved, taxcollectors had put themselves
beyond the bounds of decent society. Likewise 'sinners'
by definition fell under the condemnation of those who
were confident that they knew what righteousness was
and who found them wanting, insufficiently scrupulous
in their observance of Torah.[29] By offering friendship
and his good news to such people Jesus was deliberately
snubbing the religious conventions which evidently had
a powerful hold among his people, setting himself
against those who sought to establish the ethical and
religious tone for the wider community. Here his
freedom of attitude and action was more openly
challenging of such authority.

As for sinners on a grander scale, that is, Gentiles
and foreigners, the evidence is more mixed. Jesus
evidently did not see his own mission as directed
towards Gentiles, but only 'to the lost sheep of the
house of Israel' (Matt. 10:5–6; 15:24). But he did
respond positively to the two Gentiles who are recalled
as appealing directly to him – the centurion and the
Syro-Phoenician woman – and he evidently regarded
their faith as a model of what faith should be (Matt.
8:5–13; Mark 7:24–30). Moreover, he probably
looked for a time when Gentiles would be given a share
in the inheritance of Abraham: many from east and
west would sit at table with the patriarchs in the
kingdom of heaven (Matt. 8:11–12); and responsibility
for the vineyard of Israel would be given to others
(Mark 12:9). The most striking evidence of his unwill-
ingness to be bound by social convention on this point,

---

29 See n. 14 above.

however, is the parable of the good Samaritan (Luke 10:30–37). The fact that he chose a Samaritan as the story's hero, particularly as over against the obvious failing of the priest and Levite, representatives of the religious bureaucracy, can hardly be seen as other than a sharp critique of prevailing attitudes towards Judea's despised northern neighbour.

The third example given above was the discrimination against women taken for granted in Jewish society. Here too we need simply recall, by way of contrast, that Jesus showed himself remarkably free in his own relationships with women. There were a number of women supporters who followed him (that would be unconventional in itself), and who helped make provision for him out of their own means (Mark 15:40–41; Luke 8:2). Prominent among them was one, Mary Magdalene, a woman from whom Jesus had cast out seven demons (see also Mark 15:47; 16:1; John 19:25; 20:1–2, 11–18); also Mary and Martha (Luke 10:38–42; John 11); and several others whose names are recalled. In fact, we know the names of at least seven women remembered for their close support of Jesus – a number not so far removed from the twelve disciples! In addition, a woman, described again as a 'sinner', is recalled as causing scandal by anointing his feet and wiping them with her hair (Luke 7:37–39); and Jesus himself is remembered as rejoicing that taxcollectors and prostitutes are entering the kingdom before the chief priests and the elders of the people (Matt. 21:31–32). Such a claim would be just as shocking today! Nor should we forget that the Markan version of the divorce pericope has Jesus envisaging the equal possibility of divorce instituted by the wife as well as by the husband (Mark 10:12). It would hardly be unjust to say that at such points Jesus flew in the face of social convention.

The most striking example of his freedom in this

area, however, must be in relation to family ties.[30] It is true, as we have already noted, that he rebuked those who sat light to marriage ties and responsibilities to parents. But he is also recalled as setting the new ties of discipleship and concern for the things of the kingdom above family ties; 'whoever does the will of God is my brother, and sister, and mother' (Mark 3:31–35). According to Luke 9:59–60, he set the call of discipleship above the most fundamental of a child's family responsibilities – to provide burial for his father – a shocking dereliction of duty.[31] It is also Luke who recalls Jesus as saying: 'If anyone comes to me and does not hate his own father and mother and wife and children and brothers and sisters, yes, and even his own life, he cannot be my disciple' (Luke 14:26; cf. Matt. 10:37–38). Such sayings can readily be understood as emphasizing the sharpness of choice in hyperbolic terms. But the fact that Jesus was evidently willing to pose the challenge of the call of the kingdom in such terms remains significant. It is a further and even sharper example of his willingness to cut through issues of debate and choice to fundamental principles.

In short, here too, in the area of the authority of convention, and still more clearly than in the earlier cases, we see Jesus exercising a discriminating freedom of action and relationship. He was not bound by the conventions we have examined, conventions which formed and sustained a basic part of the social fabric. In the light of the more fundamental relationships of God's kingly rule he found it necessary to set aside and disregard them, to exercise the freedom of God's kingdom.

---

30 See S. C. Barton, *Discipleship and Family Ties according to Mark and Matthew* (Cambridge: Cambridge University, 1994).
31 See M. Hengel, *The Charismatic Leader and His Followers* (Edinburgh: T. & T. Clark, 1981) chap. 1; E. P. Sanders, *Jesus and Judaism* (London: SCM, 1985) pp. 252–5.

7. Conclusions

What then do we learn from our case study of Jesus and freedom in relation to authority? Caution must be exercised, since we cannot simply assume that Jesus provides a typical role model, or that the circumstances in which he lived and taught are paradigmatic for other times and situations. Nevertheless, the fact that the Gospels do take pains to portray Jesus in these terms,[32] and various indications in Paul[33] and elsewhere strongly suggest that such memories and material were preserved, at least in part, for their value as examples to would-be disciples of Jesus.[34] In which case, and allowing for all the problems of transposing the principles drawn from such stories and sayings into a different time and idiom, certain conclusions can be drawn which may be of wider than merely historical value.

In the first place, we must note the degree to which Jesus was willing to work within the structures of authority then prevailing – certainly the secular authority, and in large measure also the religious authority and the authority of the Torah.

He was no apostle of violent revolution; he was no anarchist. That is not to say that he was a passionate supporter or defender of such authority, simply that he worked within that authority, that he was subservient to it at critical points (supporting the payment of taxes,

32 This must be a large part of the explanation for Luke's emphasis on Jesus as a man of prayer. See e.g. B. E. Beck, *Christian Character in the Gospel of Luke* (London: Epworth, 1989) p. 118.
33 See e.g. Rom. 12:14; 13:8–10; 14:14; 15:3; 1 Cor. 13:2; Gal. 6:2; Col. 2:6; 1 Thess. 4:1; 5:2, 6.
34 We do not have time to go into the question of Jesus' expectation of an imminent coming of the kingdom of God. The Gospels show that whatever the understanding of the matter they preserve, the remembrance of Jesus' teaching and ministry was of continuing importance for the discipleship of first and second generation believers.

the continuation of the Temple offerings, and the authority of the Torah), and that he shaped his mission within its constraints.

In the second place, we see Jesus willing to exercise critical judgment in relation to such authority – to criticize a Herod, to engage in a symbolical act of judgment against the Temple, to abstract a fundamental principle from the Torah and use it to relativize other commandments. In all this we see that critical interaction with the authority of established tradition, that refusal to give servile and unquestioning obedience to 'the authorities' which we saw in the first lecture to be at the heart of liberty, of the experience of liberation and essential to sustaining the vitality of liberty.

Thirdly, we have seen how Jesus, by going back to first or fundamental principles of relationship with God and mutual relationship between men and women, exercised a far-reaching freedom in reference to many of the customs and conventions which formed the fabric of the society of his own day. The discrimination to recognize which conventions and which fundamental principles lies at the heart of his own experience and exercise of liberty.

Finally in a theme where the primary contrast is between freedom and slavery, we do well to recall that the paradoxical ideal set forth by Jesus for discipleship was *not* freedom to lord it over others, to have one's own way, to have others wait upon one's wishes, but freedom to choose the role of servant and slave (Mark 10:42–45). Freedom in the face of authority is never so clearly expressed as in the freedom of self-denial and self-sacrifice. It was this freedom which Jesus himself expressed both in his life and in his dying. Such a thought brings us to our next theme.

CHAPTER THREE

Liberty and the Self

1. Introduction

The second area we looked at in the first lecture was liberty and the self – the fact that freedom has to be not only about liberty from outward authority, but about inner freedom too. The world and its history are full of individuals who claimed and exerted a considerable degree of freedom in relation to the princes and governments of this world, their rules and decrees, or in relation to the authority of social convention, but who became enslaved to debasing habits and debilitating vices in their personal lives. What within the New Testament speaks to this theme?

The most obvious test case is that of Paul. As Jesus provided an inviting test case on the theme of liberty and authority, so it is Paul who immediately offers himself and his teaching on the theme of liberty and the self. For one thing, his own experience has served as one of the classic models of conversion – as a complete turning round from one religion to another, as a liberation from Judaism into a different system. Paul himself never thought of it quite in those terms; he saw himself rather as one called, like Isaiah and Jeremiah of old, to announce and interpret Israel's calling from God in unexpected terms and in terms his own people would not accept – commissioned within Israel, not converted from Israel. Yet, since his Damascus road experience evidently shattered the old mould of his self-understanding, belief and life-style, and gave birth to a radically different self-understanding, belief and life-style, 'conversion' is not an improper word to use.[1] So liberation there was: in his own terms, liberation within his ancestral religion, not liberation from it; but liberation nonetheless.

More to the point is the fact that of all NT writers it is Paul who uses the language of liberty and freedom more than any other. On a simple statistical survey, the Pauline corpus uses the basic vocabulary of liberty more than twice as often as the rest of the NT writers put together. Typical is his interjection in 2 Cor. 3:17 – 'Where the Spirit of the Lord is, there is freedom!' Equally characteristic is his not infrequent recourse to the metaphor of slavery – the words 'slavery' and the verbs, 'to be a slave' and 'to make a slave', being even more predominantly Pauline within NT vocabulary. Notable here, for example, is the considerable play he makes of the slavery-freedom antithesis in Romans 6 – as in 6:17–18: 'You were once slaves of sin . . . (but now) having been set free from sin, (you) have become slaves of righteousness'.

This is sufficient indication, therefore, that on any discussion of liberty in NT terms, Paul must be a primary witness. And, in particular, in a discussion on personal liberty, of liberty in relation to the passions, the disqualified mind, the darkness of self-deception, Paul is more likely than any other NT writer to provide insight of perennial value and teaching of continuing worth.

---

1 See particularly A. Segal, *Paul the Convert. The Apostolate and Apostasy of Saul the Pharisee* (New Haven: Yale University, 1990).

2. The powers that control the self

What in Paul's view are the factors which affect the self, the powers which control the self, the influences which can enslave the self? We can easily identify a number from his writings.

a) First there are what he calls 'the authorities' (*exousiai*). I use this title as shorthand for the range of powers he lists in a passage like Rom. 8:38 –

> I am sure that neither death nor life, nor angels nor rulers, neither things present nor things to come nor powers, neither height nor depth, nor any other creature will be able to separate us from the love of God which is in Christ Jesus our Lord.

The more famous list is in Eph. 6:12 –

> We are not contending against flesh and blood, but against the rulers, against the authorities, against the cosmic powers of this darkness, against the spiritual forces of evil in the heavenly places.

By 'authorities' it is clear, in some cases, that Paul has in mind the secular authorities: particularly Rom. 13:1–3 – Paul's advice to Christians in Rome on how to behave in the very seat of imperial power. In that case it would appear that Paul taught an even more consistently quietist role of good citizenship and good neighbourliness, including, once again, the payment of taxes (12:14–3.7). Thus was a highly understandable policy in an age when the reality of political power was confined to a small minority at the best of times. It is an interesting fact that Paul does not use the language of freedom in relation to these authorities. For in reality it was impossible to conceive of being free from such authority.[2]

---

2 See e.g. my *Romans* (Word Biblical Commentary 38; Dallas, Word, 1988) p. 759.

But our interest here is particularly in the equally clear indications that Paul was ready to talk of, and thus to that extent also to envisage *spiritual* authorities – angelic or demonic powers who controlled human destiny in at least some measure. Apart from the two passages already cited we need only recall, for example, his talk of 'the god of this world having blinded the minds of unbelievers, to keep them from seeing the light of the gospel of the glory of Christ' (2 Cor. 4:4), and the talk in Col. 1:13 of having been 'delivered from the dominion of darkness'. So too, in 1 Cor. he evidently envisaged demons as the reality behind idols, and talks readily of 'gods many and lords many' (10:20; 8:5). And in Gal. 4:9 he speaks of being enslaved to 'the weak and beggarly elemental forces'.[3]

It is obvious in all this that Paul is 'plugging in' to the then widespread belief in the influence of the stars and of fate in human lives – the sort of belief which is still evident today in the continuing interest in horoscopes and star charts. The extent to which Paul actually believed in the real existence of such powers is a matter of debate. The very variety of his vocabulary suggests that he himself had no firm conceptuality of the powers of evil of which he speaks, and that his concern may have been largely *ad hominem*. That is to say, in so speaking he was evidently trading on such beliefs; he was writing for those who certainly believed in such powers, and writing to calm their fears and to show how the gospel answered such fear.

For our purposes, however, the debate may be largely academic, since there are at least two clearly defined powers of which Paul speaks quite often – sin and death.

---

3 See particularly the trilogy by W. Wink, *The Powers* (Philadelphia: Fortress, 1984, 1986, 1992).

b) In Paul *sin and death* appear regularly as entities which exert real and tangible power over people. In the first case Paul takes the common concept of human sin, that is, failure to obey the divine will, or explicit breach of the divine will, often synonymous with unrighteousness or lawlessness, and does something unusual with it. He personifies it, treats it as though it were a personal power. For example, it entered the world (Rom. 5:12), it reigns over and enslaves humankind (5:21; 6:6, 12–23), it came to life, launched a surprise attack and killed him (7:8–11). Whatever the reality or unreality of spiritual powers in heavenly places, for Paul there was indeed a power which was all too real, a power which manifested itself in multiple instances of human weakness, in failure to achieve the good and of desire for what is bad.

In a very similar way Paul takes the word death – as today, the word used for the expiry of human life – and personifies it also, though in this case Paul's usage has more precedents.[4] Death too can be said to reign (Rom. 5:14, 17; 6:9); it is listed as one of the powers in Rom. 8:38; and in the unforgettable language of 1 Cor. 15 death is described as 'the last enemy' and in OT language challenged to demonstrate its victory (15:26, 54–56). In both cases we might well be tempted to speak of Paul's 'existentialist demythologizing' of the talk of spiritual powers. The powers he is really and most consistently concerned about are the powers whose influence is all too obvious – that power opposed to God, whatever it is, which brings about human sinfulness, and that power which brings all human life to an end. Whatever other powers may be in question, the power of sin and death certainly exercises clear and baneful influence over the self.

---

4 Paul's language in Rom. 5:12 is particularly close to that of Wisd. Sol. 2:23–24.

Moreover, they do it in fearful combination: 'sin reigns in death' (Rom 5:21); 'sin came to life, and I died ... sin producing death' (7:9, 13); 'the sting of death is sin' (1 Cor. 15:56). That is what makes death itself so fearful, and not simply a natural falling asleep at the end of life; death as the product of sin, death as the outworking of sin's rule, death as a poisoned chalice put into our hands by sin.

c) But what is it that gives sin and death such a hold over the self, so that Paul can speak of the self as enslaved by sin? The answer is summed up in the two words, *flesh and desire*. In Paul flesh is not itself conceived as a spiritual power; nor does he think of it as sinful in itself. Flesh simply denotes human belongingness to this world – not just physicality, but typified by physicality. It signifies human weakness and mortality – the flesh that quickly tires each day, is subject to illness and disease and eventually decays back into the dust. It signifies human dependence on the world for identity and recognition, and for satisfaction of its animal instincts. And so it also comes to signify a life focussed in upon itself, the life of the flesh as a life of anxious self-seeking (see e.g. Rom. 13:14; 1 Cor. 15:50; 2 Cor. 4:11; 12:7; Gal. 4:13; 5:13).[5]

It is this weakness and dependence which enables sin to exert its power through the flesh. The classic text is Rom. 7:14ff.:

> I am a man of flesh, sold under sin. For I do not know what I do. For that which I commit is not what I want; but what I hate I do. ... But now it is no longer I doing this but sin which dwells within me. For I know

---

5 See e.g. W. D. Stacey, *The Pauline View of Man* (London: Macmillan, 1956) chap. 11; H.Ridderbos, *Paul. An Outline of his Theology* (Grand Rapids: Eerdmans; 1975/London: SPCK, 1977) pp. 93–5.

that there dwells in me, that is, in my flesh, no good
thing . . .

Sin is able to manipulate the flesh particularly in
relation to the 'desires' (*epithumiai*). 'Desire' in Paul
can be something neutral: in 1 Thess. 2:17, for
example, he speaks of his great desire to see his readers.
But the concept is more common in Paul in a negative
sense, the merely animal appetites, desire for what is
forbidden, passion. Passion, we may say, is desire
corrupted into selfish desire, token of the self's enslavement to sin. Characteristic of Paul is his call to the
Romans 'not to let sin rule in your mortal body to obey
its desires' (6:12); or his reminder, 'When we were in
the flesh the sinful passions . . . were effective in what
we are and do so as to bear fruit for death' (7:5); or his
later exhortation, 'Make no provision for the flesh, to
gratify its desires' (13:14).

d) Finally we must mention the *law*. This appears
in many of the texts just reviewed as a further factor.

> 'The law came in to increase the trespass' (Rom. 5.20);
> 'the sinful passions aroused by the law' (Rom. 7:5);
> 'God has done what the law, weakened by the flesh,
> could not do' (Rom. 8:3); 'the sting of death is sin, and
> the power of sin is the law' (1 Cor. 15:56).

Many assume from this that Paul envisages the law also
as a spiritual, heavenly power. And there is a sense in
which this is true, at least in Galatians. For there
Paul links the law with the concept of a nation's
guardian angels: the law was a kind of slave supervisor
(*paidagogos*) over Israel during Israel's minority;[6]
consequently for Gentile Christians to want to obey the

---

6 As has recently been stressed, the metaphor of the *paidagogos* was not
essentially a negative one; see e.g. R. N. Longenecker, *Galatians* (Word
Biblical Commentary 41; Dallas: Word, 1990) pp. 146–8.

law was tantamount to their wanting to put themselves once again under the rule of their old gods, the elemental forces (Gal. 3:19, 24; 4:8–10). Hence Paul's cry in Gal. 5:1, 'For freedom Christ has set us free; stand fast therefore and do not submit again to a yoke of slavery'; where the law is clearly being thought of as an enslaving power.

But in Romans the law is 'let off the hook'. The law only seems to be a principal player in the enslavement of humankind. The reality is that the law has been used by sin. Sin is the real culprit. Hence again the classic treatment in Rom. 7: 'Is the law sin? Certainly not! . . . (It was) sin, (which) seizing its opportunity through the commandment, deceived me and through it killed me' (7:7, 11). The law, like humankind itself, has been duped by sin. 'For we know that the law is spiritual; but I am fleshly . . .' (7:14). And so unfolds what is actually more a defence of the law than anything else. Yet even in Romans Paul speaks of being 'under the law' (Rom. 6:14) in the same way that he speaks of being 'under sin' (Rom. 3:9). So even in Romans the thought of the law as an oppressive power is still present.

The problem of the law for Paul focusses in Israel. The typical Jew of his day regarded the law given by God to Israel as a great gift and privilege. This law, God's law, marked out Israel as special to God, as his own people, and as such, distinct from the other nations. An early expression of this is Deut. 32:8–9: God appointed the nations their inheritance, and gave guardian angels in charge of them; but Israel he kept for himself. The law, then, is a mark of God's special favour to Israel, to show Israel how to walk in his ways as his people (the principal theme of Deut). Similar is the thought of divine Wisdom identified with the law; what all the nations seek but cannot find God has given to Israel in the law. 'Turn, O Jacob, and take her . . .

Do not give your glory to another, or your advantages to an alien people. Happy are we, O Israel, for we know what is pleasing to God' (Bar. 4:2–4). The sentiment is just that which Paul attributes to the 'Jew' in Rom. 2:17ff. – 'you are called a "Jew" and rely on the law and boast in God, and know his will . . .'. The consequence, however, was that those outside the law, without law, were thereby deemed to be also outside the sweep of God's covenant grace to Israel – in the words of Eph. 2:12, 'separated from Christ, alienated from the commonwealth of Israel, strangers to the covenants of promise, having no hope and without God in the world'.

It is this attitude, I would suggest, which Paul has primarily in view in his critique of the law as a spiritual power. To regard the law as thus 'over' Israel is in effect to treat it as itself a spiritual power – Israel's guardian angel against sin and talisman against death. But in fact the law so regarded becomes the instrument of sin, rather than a fence against sin. For it ties the Israel of God tightly to the flesh – the flesh of Abraham – that is, to physical descent from Abraham; it defines righteousness in terms first and foremost of ethnic identity – that which the devout 'Jew' does, that which in principle is possible only for 'the circumcised' (hence Rom. 2:25–29; 4:1ff.; 9:6–9); Jews can even be called simply 'the circumcision' (not the circumcised) because their identity is so much focussed in this Torah requirement in the flesh (Gal. 2:7–9; Phil. 3:3). In this way the law encourages a presumptuousness of Jewish privilege and boasting which is like Adam's first presumptuousness in seeking to know good and evil for himself. This explains why, inter alia, Rom. 7:7–12 can be understood both in terms of Adam and of Israel: the 'I' who is seduced by sin to desire what is contrary to God's will is both Adam lusting after the forbidden fruit and Israel lusting after a place of privilege in God's

affections clearly marked out by the law.[7] It also helps
explain why in 2 Cor. 3 Paul can describe the old
dispensation of Moses as one of condemnation and
death; for it is precisely the law as *gramma* ('letter')
which kills, that is, the law regarded both as a first
principle like the elemental forces in Galatians, and as
something outward and visible, leaving its mark in the
flesh (cf. Rom. 2:29).

In short, in Paul's way of understanding things,
there are two powers which can be said to control
human existence, to enslave humankind: these are sin
and death. Whatever other powers there may or may
not be, the reality of sin and death and of the sway of
sin and death over humanity is not to be disputed.
Their power is made possible by the weakness of
humanity, its fleshliness, the decay of mortality, the
dependence on that which is not God for satisfaction of
appetites and desires. Sin has also been able to use the
law, particularly Israel's over-dependence on the law,
to tie the bonds of sin and death even more tightly on
flesh-focussed humanity.

That being the case, in what sense can it be said
that the gospel sets the believer free – free from sin and
death? free from the flesh and its desires? free from the
law? We begin by looking at the first two together.
Does Paul think that the believer has been freed from
sin, death and flesh? And if so, in what sense?

3.   Free from sin, death and flesh

a) It is certainly the case that Paul does think of the
believer as having been freed from the power of sin,

---

7 The disagreement among commentators on this question (does Rom.
7:7–12 reflect an Adam or an Israel background?) should therefore not be
posed as a straightforward either-or; see e.g. my *Romans* pp. 379–85.

death and the flesh in some sense. Rom. 6–8 are in fact a treatment of this very theme. As already noted, in Rom. 6 Paul says so explicitly in reference to sin: 'you have been set free from sin . . . and have become slaves of God' (6:18, 22); and at the beginning he stated equally clearly, 'We have died to sin' (6:2). In some sense it is true also of the flesh – believers are free from the flesh; thus Rom. 7 begins with the analogy of being freed from a relationship by death, and goes on to characterize the old relationship as living in the flesh – 'When we were living in the flesh, our sinful passions . . . bore fruit for death' – the implication being that the believer is no longer 'in the flesh' in that sense, is free from the flesh. In some sense the same is also true of death – the believer is free of death; thus again in Rom. 8: 'The law of the Spirit of life in Christ Jesus has set me free from the law of sin and death' (Rom. 8:2). Influential here has been Nygren's commentary on *Romans*, in which he characterized the theme of these chapters in terms of freedom – freedom from sin, freedom from the law, freedom from death.[8]

But it also notable that there is a certain rhythm in these same chapters. Paul begins by speaking thus in clear-cut terms: you have died to sin; you have been set free; and so on. But then he immediately goes on to exhort his readers in terms which indicate with almost equal clarity that the relationship with sin, flesh and death is by no means at an end for believers. Thus in chapter 6, the second half is dominated by the plea *not* to let sin have any say in their lives:

> Do not let sin rule in your mortal body to obey its desires, and do not give sin control of what you are and do as weapons of unrighteousness. But give God decisive control of yourselves as being alive from the

---

8 A. Nygren, *Commentary on Romans* (London: SCM, 1952) p. 188.

dead and of what you are and do to God as weapons of
righteousness (6:12–13).

If Paul really believed that Christians were free from the
power of sin, how could he so exhort them? The power
of sin is evidently still a power to be reckoned with by
the believer, a power to be resisted. The war of
liberation is by no means finally won.

Likewise in chapter 7, Paul goes on to speak of his
continuing fleshliness, and ends with the sobering
summary, 'So then I myself with my mind serve the law
of God and with my flesh the law of sin' (7:25). It
would appear that there is a dimension of his being,
even as a believer, which is still 'in the flesh', still
subservient to its desires. The point is disputed, but this
acknowledgment of a continuing subserviency of the
flesh appears to be the qualification of the strong
opening assertions of chapter 7, equivalent to the
qualifications of the strong opening assertions in
chapters 6 and 8.[9]

Likewise in Chapter 8, Paul has no sooner said,
'You are not in the flesh but in the Spirit, assuming that
the Spirit of God does indeed dwell in you', when he
goes on:

> So then, brothers, we are under no obligation to the
> flesh to live in accordance with the flesh. For if you live
> in accordance with the flesh, you will certainly die; but
> if by the Spirit you put to death the deeds of the body,
> you will live (8:9, 12–13).

Here again the issue seems to be much more in the
balance than the initial optimism suggested. The flesh is
not simply a factor belonging to the past; its influence
could still be crucial. And death too still threatens as a
power; or at least Paul is able to threaten his readers

---

9 See my *Romans* pp. 301–3.

with its power. Even as Christians they can be warned, 'If you live in accordance with the flesh, you will certainly die'!

b) What are we to make of this? Paul is certainly ready to talk about the freedom of the Christian in relation to sin, death and flesh. But, equally clearly, it is a qualified freedom. In what sense, then, are believers free from these powers and conditions? To answer we must start from what has been called for some time now the 'Already/Not yet' tension in Paul's understanding of salvation.[10] That is to say, salvation for Paul is a process, not a once-for-all event; Christians by definition are 'those who are in the process of being saved' (1 Cor. 1:18; 2 Cor. 2:15), not those who are (already) saved. The process has *begun*; that is the 'already' element in his teaching. But the process has *still to be completed*; that is the 'not yet' element in his teaching. He speaks in just these terms, for example, in Phil. 1:6 – 'I am sure that he who began a good work in you (the 'already') will bring it to completion at the day of Jesus Christ' (the 'not yet'). And the argument in Galatians is precisely about getting the right balance between the beginning event (the 'already') and the continuing process (the 'not yet').[11]

Returning to Rom. 6–8, we can see how this already/not yet tension works out in his treatment of sin, death and flesh. Thus in Rom. 6 he begins by talking about believers as having died with Christ, 'baptized into his death' (6:3–4), where the once-for-

---

10 Justifiably influential here has been O. Cullmann, *Christ and Time. The Primitive Christian Conception of Time and History* (London: SCM; revised 1962).

11 For fuller exposition see my 'The Theology of Galatians: The Issue of Covenantal Nomism', *Pauline Theology Vol. I*, ed. J. M. Bassler (Minneapolis: Fortress, 1991) pp. 125–46, here pp. 131–2; also my *The Theology of Paul's Letter to the Galatians* (Cambridge: Cambridge University, 1993).

all-pastness of the Greek aorist tense is prominent; that is the already. But then he changes the metaphor slightly: 'For if we have become knit together with the very likeness of his death, we shall certainly also be knit together with the very likeness of his resurrection' (6:5). What is significant here is that the tense changes, from aorist to perfect and future. The point of the perfect is to indicate a continuing state which results from a past action; and the future we might call the 'not yet' tense. So here Paul envisages believers as in some sense still bonded with Christ's death, and awaiting a still future bonding with his resurrection. The point is the same in Gal. 2:19, where Paul again uses the perfect tense when he claims, 'I have been crucified with Christ' – that is, I was nailed with Christ to the cross, and am still hanging there with him!

Here is a first key factor in Paul's understanding of Christian freedom. It is a *process* which begins by individual believers identifying themselves with Christ in his death (through baptism). That in itself is a transition from one state to another and in itself it merits the description of 'liberation' (the already). But whereas Christ himself has died once for all and is now free from any claim of sin on him (Rom. 6:9–10), believers' identification with Christ in his death is an ongoing event, and their identification with Christ in his resurrection still lies in the future (the not yet). The believer is somehow caught in suspense between Good Friday and Easter Sunday. The process of metamorphosis into the image of God in Christ is a life-long one.[12] That is why Paul elsewhere can speak so movingly about the inevitable necessity of believers sharing in Christ's sufferings. Thus in the example of Rom. 8:17 – 'heirs together with Christ, provided that we suffer with him in order that we might also be glorified with

---

12 Note the present tenses in Rom. 12:2 and 2 Cor. 3:18.

him'; or in Phil. 3:10–11 – 'I want to know Christ and
the power of his resurrection, and the sharing of his
sufferings by becoming like him in his death, that if
possible I may attain the resurrection from the dead'.

A second key factor is the *flesh* itself – implicit in
Paul's talk of his continuing fleshliness in Rom. 7 and
of the danger of living a flesh-dominated life in Rom. 8.
For it is self-evident that the flesh simply *cannot* cease
to be a factor in the life of believers. Paul indicates this
clearly enough by talking of his own continuing life 'in
the flesh' on more than one occasion (Gal. 2:20; Phil.
1:22). Consequently it is cheap theology to take his talk
of believers' *past* life 'in the flesh' as implying that as
believers they are no longer 'in the flesh'. The point is
that Paul sees salvation as a salvation of the whole
person – body as well. So until this body, the body of
flesh, the mortal body has died or been transformed
salvation is incomplete. In the meantime the process
of death is incomplete, and therefore to that extent at
least the rule of death is not yet broken. So again in
Rom. 8 –

> If Christ is in you, the body is dead because of sin . . .
> But if the Spirit of him who raised Jesus from the dead
> dwells in you, he who raised Christ from the dead will
> give life to your mortal bodies as well, through his
> Spirit which dwells in you (8:11).

This passage points to the third key factor – the
Spirit. It is typical of Paul's teaching here that the gift of
the Spirit is what begins the believer's new relation with
God through Christ. The Spirit is precisely the Spirit of
'adoption', the Spirit that makes us sons and daughters
of God, sharing in Christ's sonship (8:14–17). In an
alternative metaphor, the Spirit is the first-fruits of the
final harvest of salvation, that is, the first sheaf of the
reaping, the beginning of the process of harvesting itself
– but only the beginning. The process thus begun must

await completion in the completion of the harvest, that is, the harvest of resurrection. Hence the character of the in-between time is one of often groaning tension: 'Also we ourselves, who have the first-fruits of the Spirit, we also ourselves groan within ourselves, eagerly awaiting adoption, the redemption of our body' (8:23). Striking here is the way Paul, within a few verses of each other, can use the same metaphor, that of adoption, for both of the main phases in the process of salvation – both for its beginning (receiving the Spirit of adoption) and for its end (the adoption, that is, the redemption of our bodies). The process of salvation is one of ongoing tension between these two adoptions, or two phases of the one complete adoption.[13]

c) Where then is freedom?, we may ask again. Where is the freedom of the Christian? At first sight the answer seems to be, Nowhere. Far from being completely free, the believer is still in the flesh, still awaiting the outworking of death's rule, still to that extent, at least, 'under sin'. Far from being free, the believer seems rather to be caught in a state of tension, of incompleteness, where the joy of the already is quickly overshadowed by the groaning of the not yet. Indeed, it seems to be a state of almost open warfare, where, in the words of Gal. 5:17, 'what the flesh desires is opposed to the Spirit, and what the Spirit desires is opposed to the flesh; for these are opposed to each other, to prevent you from doing what you want.' Not much freedom here. And yet Paul does speak of freedom, even in these circumstances. It is precisely as part of his exposition of Christian freedom, ('You were called to freedom, brothers' – 5:13) that Paul goes on to speak of the continuing tension and warfare between

---

13 See my *Jesus and the Spirit. A Study of the Religious and Charismatic Experience of Jesus and the First Christians as Reflected in the New Testament* (London: SCM/Philadelphia: Westminster, 1975) pp. 308–42.

flesh and Spirit (so also in Rom. 8:1–13). What freedom is he thinking of?

We may be sure that it is not a merely symbolical freedom, as though the believer after baptism and the gift of the Spirit was no more free than before. Nor, we may be equally sure, has Paul any thought of a second experience of the Spirit, sanctification, second blessing, baptism in the Spirit, or whatever, which secures freedom from sin or flesh or death. There is no indication whatsoever that Paul envisaged an experience of complete liberation from the flesh, or its oppressors, this side of death. To be sure, he admits to 'out of the body' experiences himself (2 Cor. 12), but only to make the point that the thorn in the flesh soon brought him down to earth with a bump, an experience which taught Paul to glory in his weakness, not in any escape from weakness (12:7–10). So our question still stands, What freedom?

The answer is best taken in three parts. First, it is *the freedom of a decisive commitment made*, itself rooted in the once-for-all action of God in Christ's death and resurrection. It is thus the freedom of those who are not still anxiously wondering about where their first loyalty should lie, but who have made the great choice which relativizes and determines all other choices. The die has been cast. Now it is a matter of living in the light of these decisive events and in the strength which they continue to give. The homing pigeon no longer need circle round anxiously; it has found the direction it must fly and is free to do so. It is the freedom which comes when the great question of life has been settled, and only secondary questions remain.

Second, it is *the freedom of dependency on God*, and no longer of dependency on sin and the flesh for identity and value, no longer dependency on what decays and dies for meaning and purpose. 'Having been

set free from sin, you have become slaves of righteousness' (Rom. 6:18). Notice that this freedom is not an
escape from slavery. That is the old will-o'-the-wisp –
for humankind to think that it *can* be free, independent,
autonomous. Not so. Never so! The human being can
never escape from a state of dependency on things and
relationships. The question then is simply whether it is
a dependency which binds us closer to sin, flesh and
death; or a dependency on a higher power, the power
which makes it possible for us to be what we were
made to be and which little by little moulds us into
what we were made to be, the image of God in
Christ. The latter is what Paul certainly has in mind,
and that he regards as freedom – only the *beginning* of
the freedom of the children of God, but freedom
nonetheless.

Thirdly it is *the freedom of acknowledged self-
weakness*, a weakness which does not think to stand or
prosper on the basis of its own resources, but only on
those from God. It is a weakness, therefore, which
is free indeed, free from the self in its various
manifestations – self-gratification, self-assertion, self-
justification, self-pity, and so on – because in the end all
is of God. This presumably is precisely why Paul
climaxes his description of the divided individual in
Rom. 7 with his cry, 'Wretched man that I am! Who
will deliver me from this body of death', and his
response, 'Thanks be to God through Jesus Christ our
Lord!' (Rom. 7:24–25). This is precisely why he
climaxes his description of the work of the Spirit in the
believer with the description of the prayer which is
successful before God just because it is the prayer of
weakness, the prayer where we do not even know what
to say and can manage to utter only wordless groans
(Rom. 8:26).

In short, the freedom Paul has in mind, is the
freedom which grows out of a deeply rooted commit-

ment and passion, the freedom which is sustained and shaped by deep resources of the divine Spirit within the human spirit, the freedom which lives by the sign of the cross as the paradigm for life still to be lived in this world. This is what Paul seems to mean when he speaks of freedom from sin and death and in relation to the flesh. But what about the other member of the dreadful triumvirate – sin, death and law? This is the one outstanding member of the forces which control the self which we have yet to consider. What does Paul mean by freedom in this case?

4. Freedom from the law

Paul's teaching on the law is one of the most disputed areas of Pauline theology at present, and there is hardly scope here to deal with it adequately.[14] But if the earlier analysis is at all to the point we can summarize Paul's teaching on freedom from the law in something like the following terms.

a) In the first place we can certainly speak of *freedom from the condemnation of the law*. 'There is therefore now no condemnation for those who are in Christ Jesus; (they have been) set free from the law of sin and death' (Rom. 8:1). Paul will have in mind several factors here: the function of the law in bringing definition and knowledge of sin (Rom. 3:20; 5:13); the law as 'bringing about wrath' (Rom. 4:15), that is, expressing and thus bringing to effect God's judgment and condemnation of transgression; and above all, the

---

14 For bibliography and review of the discussion see my *Romans* pp. lxiii-lxiv; D. Moo, 'Paul and the Law in the Last Ten Years', *Scottish Journal of Theology* 40 (1987) pp. 287–307; S. Westerholm, *Israel's Law and the Church's Faith. Paul and his Recent Interpreters* (Grand Rapids: Eerdmans, 1988);

law used by sin to mislead the sinner into the very transgression it condemns by highlighting the weakness of the flesh and the strength of human desire (Rom. 7:8–11). To what extent, then, has the believer been freed from this condemnation of the law? Since the condemnation is condemnation of sin, and since sin manipulates the law to increase transgression, the answer must be: To the extent that believers have been freed from the power of sin, to that extent have they been freed from the condemnation of the law.

To be more specific. According to Rom. 8:3, freedom from the law's condemnation is achieved by Christ, sent in the very likeness of sinful flesh and as a sacrifice for sin, himself condemning sin in the flesh. That is, Christ's death as a man of sinful flesh was in effect the sin offering which by its death destroyed the flesh through which sin maintained its power over humanity.[15] Freedom from condemnation, therefore, is bound up, in Paul's thinking, with the theology of the sin offering: the sinner identifying as sinner with the sin-offering, so that its destruction dealt with the sinner's sin, and thus removed the ground of condemnation.[16] So the believer, by identifying with Christ in his sacrificial death likewise escapes condemnation. But, as we have already seen, this identification with Christ in his death is caught between the Already and the Not yet. Consequently the freedom from condemnation itself is caught in the same suspense: as already in Christ, the believer is freed from condemnation; as not yet free of the flesh, the believer is still under the threat of condemnation.

b) In the second place we can speak of *freedom*

---

15 See e.g. N. T. Wright, *The Climax of the Covenant. Christ and the Law in Pauline Theology* (Edinburgh: T. & T. Clark, 1991) pp. 220–5.
16 See my 'Paul's Understanding of the Death of Jesus as Sacrifice', *Sacrifice and Redemption. Durham Essays in Theology*, ed. S. W. Sykes (Cambridge: Cambridge University, 1991) pp. 35–56.

from the law itself. That is, freedom from the law as a spiritual power, as defined above. That is, in the terms used by Galatians, freedom from a state of under-age minority, into the status of the son attaining his majority. That means for Paul, freedom to recognize that the law in its function of protecting Israel is no longer required. And that means, in turn, freedom from those specific laws which expressed and maintained Israel's difference and distinctiveness from the other nations – precisely those requirements which Paul's Galatian opponents were seeking to press on Paul's Gentile converts – circumcision in particular. It was just this demand, that these distinctively Jewish laws (circumcision, food laws, special days) were essential for those who wanted to stake a claim in Abraham's inheritance, which Paul saw as forcing Gentiles back into a status of tutelage and enslavement to the elemental forces.[17]

Here too we need to qualify the point and to tie it in to what has previously been said. For the entry into the freedom of sonship is also caught in the Already-Not yet tension. Although they have received the Spirit, the Spirit of the Son, Gentile believers have not yet entered into the full freedom of sonship. To that extent, therefore, Christians *in via* are still in the same state as Jews still living under the law. The difference is, once again, the decisive event of Christ, which has achieved a genuine degree of freedom in relation to life still under the tutelage of the law. Nevertheless, the freedom from the law is relative and not absolute, so long as life continues in the flesh.

c) It follows, in the third place, that we can speak of *freedom from the self-deception which sin uses the*

---

17 This last sentence represents an understanding of Paul's theology at this point which has developed through the essays published in *Jesus, Paul and the Law*, my commentary on *Romans*, and my forthcoming commentary on *Galatians* (London: Black, 1993).

law to achieve. The self-deception Paul has in mind is not, as usually assumed, the presumption that the law can be fully obeyed, when complete obedience in fact is impossible;[18] we need to remind ourselves that Paul expects the just requirements of the law to be fulfilled by those who walk in accordance with the Spirit (Rom. 8:4), and maintains that the whole law is fulfilled in the love command (Gal. 5:14). Nor was the self-deception any widespread belief on the part of Jews that they were sinless; on the contrary, the sacrificial system and Day of Atonement ritual catered precisely for sins; and Paul was able to claim that as a Pharisee he had been blameless (Phil. 3:6), presumably because he had used the means of grace and forgiveness provided by the cult to cover his sins.

The self-deception was rather that because they were 'within the law' their sins did not count so seriously as the sins of those who sinned outside the law. This is the self-deception which Paul attacks in Rom. 2 – the self-deception which condemned the sins of Gentiles, but which assumed that the same sins committed by themselves would be regarded less seriously – an assumption of favoured nation status which Paul describes as hardness of heart (Rom. 2:5). It is the self deception which we see expressed at times in both the Wisdom and Psalms of Solomon, both echoed in Rom. 2 – the assumption that God looked at Israel's failings more tolerantly, that the sins of Gentiles merited wrath and destruction, while those of Israel received only the discipline of a father to his son.[19] That was the self-deception which Paul likened to the serpent's deception of Adam. In contrast, believers

---

18 So, e.g., H. Hübner, *Law in Paul's Thought* (Edinburgh: T. & T. Clark, 1984) pp. 38–41.

19 See further my 'Yet Once More – "The Works of the Law": A Response', *Journal for the Study of the New Testament* 46 (1992) pp. 99–117, particularly pp. 106–9.

should have no doubt of the seriousness of their sin – 'all have sinned and fall short of the glory of God' (Rom. 3:23). But the cross provides the sufficient atonement, since it deals not just with the sin but with sin in the flesh.

d) Finally, we can speak of *freedom to obey the law*. This again is the clear implication of the passage from which we started this section. Rom. 8:1–4 – 'set free from the law of sin and death, . . . in order that the requirement of the law might be fulfilled in us who walk not in accordance with the flesh but in accordance with the Spirit'. It is the implication also of 2 Cor. 3:3, with its echo of Jer. 31:33 – the law written on the heart.[20] Again, it is also the implication of understanding the gift of the Spirit as the circumcision of the heart (Rom. 2:28–29; Phil. 3:3), and indeed also of Paul's talk of 'the obedience of faith' and of faith as establishing the law (Rom. 1:5; 3:31). The point is, that as the coming of faith (in Christ) gives a new perspective on the law which liberates both from a slave-like tutelage under the law and from a false perspective on the law, so the coming of the Spirit enables an obedience to the law from the heart, an inner motivation and discernment, not a rule-book mentality.

Put another way, it is freedom to obey the law through obedience to the love command. That command, Paul is quite clear, sums up the law; truly to love the neighbour as oneself is to fulfil the law. Not altogether surprisingly, that is the freedom which Jesus himself expressed and lived out. So our theme here begins to overlap with that of the second lecture and we need only refer back to that. But it also points forward to the fourth lecture. So we need say no more at this point.

---

20 See e.g. V. P. Furnish, *II Corinthians* (Anchor Bible 32A; New York: Doubleday, 1984) pp. 183–5:

In short, the freedom from the law of which Paul speaks can be summed up under these four heads, as freedom from the condemnation of the law, freedom from the law in its role as childhood governor, freedom from the self-deception in which the law has a part, and freedom to obey the law. The variation and the nuance are such that it is no wonder that many students of Paul have found the subject both confused and confusing.

5. Conclusions

So we can speak of a real Christian liberty in this area too. It is not the freedom spoken of in the old Greek proverb and ideal – freedom to live as one chooses, the liberty of self-sufficiency. For the Christian consciousness expressed by Paul is a consciousness of the weakness of the flesh and of the power of desire, a consciousness of the not yet of the salvation process, a consciousness that the full inheritance of the freedom of the children of God lies still in the future. Nor is it the freedom envisaged by John Stuart Mill, the freedom of the rational man confident in his rationality. For Paul was all too well aware that the human mind can be darkened, that those who think they are wise can thereby simply demonstrate what great fools they are (Rom. 1:22; 1 Cor. 1:20).

We can however speak of the freedom of self-knowledge, another ancient Greek ideal. We can do this so long as we realize that for Paul this means the freedom of knowing oneself to be a creature of the Creator, the freedom of human beings who know that they were not made to be independent, who acknowledge that the psychological and social reality of human beings is that they can never be truly independent, and who find their true freedom in a relation of dependence on God. The freedom of which Paul speaks, then, is the freedom of those who know they have been released from the self-deception of thinking they could be independent, freedom from the self-deception of thinking they were really free of the desires of the flesh or the power of sin and death, or the constraint of the law. It is the freedom of recognizing our true nature as human beings, our several and continuing weaknesses and vulnerabilities, that however far we are along the road of life we are still *in via*. In short, it is freedom from the self – freedom from the crushing responsibility of trying to manage on our own, freedom from the assumption that our social identity or our standing and reputation before others is more important than our standing before God, freedom from anxiety to have to prove ourselves and from fear of other peoples' opinions – in a word, freedom in God and from the world.

Above all, however, it is the freedom of the already, the freedom of the great transaction brought into effect by God in Christ, and particularly for Paul, the freedom of the Spirit. It is a freedom characterized precisely *not* by the law, but rather by the experience of one from whose eyes the scales of earlier devotion to the law have dropped away. It is the freedom of recognizing the directness and immediacy of the relation with God made possible by the Spirit of Christ, the freedom of a deeply rooted passion and inner spontaneity of love, thus enabled to discern the things that matter and to sit lightly to the things that are indifferent. It is the freedom to walk by the Spirit and to be led by the Spirit, the freedom of faith working through love. No wonder, then, that F. F. Bruce could entitle his major study of Paul, *Apostle of the Free Spirit*;[21] for 'where the Spirit of the Lord is, there is freedom'!

---

21 Exeter: Paternoster, 1977.

CHAPTER FOUR

Liberty and Community

1. Introduction

The third and final area which called for consideration
in the first lecture was that of liberty and society. This
is an unavoidable topic, because it is precisely where
the other two liberties, liberty from authority, and
liberty in relation to the self, come into conflict. For
authority has to be exercised for the purpose of
maintaining society. Without the authority of a duly
constituted governing body, without the bonding effect
of commonly accepted authoritative tradition, no
community can hold together for long or in good order.
And yet, it is precisely such authority which the
individual in his or her freedom must at times oppose
and resist and break through, otherwise the conser-
vatism of institutions and traditions becomes pro-
gressively more stifling and restrictive. This is Mill's
repeated concern. Yet again, individual liberty given
free reign almost inevitably becomes destructive of
society, destructive of the freedoms of other members
of society without which it cannot be called a truly free
society. So the key question remains: how to achieve a
society which provides the necessary framework of

authority and bonding tradition, while at the same time allowing sufficient individual freedom for necessary innovation and change, while at the same time safeguarding the freedom of all its members?

Our question is particularly appropriate for the beginnings of Christianity. For, as already noted,[1] Christianity began precisely as a movement questioning established authority and tradition, and which consequently found it necessary to deal with the correlation of individual freedom and the good of the society or community as a whole. The questioning did not become radical at once. Jesus, as we have seen, remained within the structures of second Temple Judaism, though his questioning of particular traditions did pose issues and point up principles which came more strongly to the fore within a few decades. But once again it was Paul in particular with whom the questioning took a form which was seen to undermine the old authority of Jewish practice and tradition. And once again it was he who wrestled most creatively with the resulting tension between liberty and community. So it is Paul who provides our third test case as he did our second.

As before we have insufficient time for a thorough analysis. But there is one passage in which more than any other Paul attempts to reconcile the two conflicting principles of orderly society and individual freedom. That is Rom. 14:1–15:6. And since we have not so far been able to go into much detailed exegesis of particular passages, but have had to be content with more sweeping overviews, it will be appropriate for this last lecture to devote ourselves to a more thoroughgoing analysis of at least one key passage. But first, in order

---

1 See above p. 25.

to tune in to Paul's wavelength we must begin by setting the passage in context.[2]

2. The historical context

Part of the value of studying Paul's letter to the Christians in Rome on this topic is that Rome was, of course, the capital city of a huge Empire. It is therefore a context in which questions about society and community are particularly relevant, and where questions of individual liberty within an authoritative framework are particularly pertinent.

The character of the Rome of which we speak is still evident in the majestic ruins and artefacts, the literature and inscriptions from the period. It was a surprisingly modern city, thoroughly cosmopolitan, with about one million residents and an unknown number of slaves; the ratio of slave to free is usually reckoned at about 1:3. Within its already sprawling quarters there were about 40,000 or 50,000 Jews, mostly living across the Tiber, in modern Trastevere. According to Philo, most of the Jews of Rome were 'Roman citizens emancipated' (*Legatio* 155); that is, they were descendants of freedmen, the Jewish slaves brought to Rome by Pompey following his conquest of Palestine in 62BC who had been manumitted thereafter and granted citizen rights at the same time.

We also know something of their social organization, having names of some ten to thirteen synagogues, all of which may have existed at this time. Each of them seems to have been regarded as an independent unit, the equivalent, for the purposes of laws governing rights of assembly, of a *collegium* or club. These rights

---

2 The details of what follows are drawn principally from my *Romans* pp. xliv–liv, to which reference can be made for fuller information.

of assembly were something watched over suspiciously by the authorities in the imperial capital – for obvious reasons. Julius Caesar had exempted synagogues when he had dissolved the *collegia*, and Augustus had evidently ratified these rights in turn. But in 41, just about a decade and a half before Paul's letter, we hear of Claudius withdrawing Jewish rights of assembly, probably for a temporary period, because the Jews were becoming too numerous. In short, the position of the Jewish community in Rome at this time seems to have been rather precarious. Large in number, but without a central organization (no ethnarch, as in Alexandria), and so rather fragmented and vulnerable to the political whims and suspicions of the secular authorities.

We have no idea when the gospel of Messiah Jesus reached Rome, but Christianity in Rome almost certainly must have begun with Jewish merchants and travellers explaining and evangelizing within the synagogue communities, and no doubt it extended more widely in the usual way, through Gentile God-fearers and proselytes. The most striking evidence is the famous passage from Suetonius, that Claudius 'expelled Jews from Rome because of their constant disturbances at the instigation of Chrestus' (*Claudius* 25.4), where more or less all agree that by Chrestus he means Christ, that is Jesus. The strong likelihood, then, is that Suetonius was referring to disturbances within the synagogues caused by Jewish reaction to the claims made by Christian Jews regarding the Christ. This ties in well with the record in Acts 18.2 that Priscilla and Aquila had to leave Rome at this time because of Claudius's decree.

The indications are, therefore, that Christianity began within the fairly independent synagogues of Rome, and that it soon caused some friction in at least some of them, sufficient to attract the attention of the authorities and for Claudius to expel at least the ring leaders, including Christian Jews like Priscilla and Aquila. This happened only about six years before Paul wrote. In that intervening six years the Christian house groups may well have become predominantly Gentile, and the Christian Jews who had been able to remain would presumably have been anxious not to cause trouble or to draw attention to themselves. This suggests in turn that the leadership of the Christian house churches would have become predominantly Gentile, and that, as Christian Jews began to return to Rome in larger numbers (with the lapse of Claudius' decree), there would be the danger of renewed tension within the synagogue communities and within the Christian groups themselves – tension, that is, between those Christians who saw the new movement still as an intra-synagogue society, and those Christians in house churches more predominantly Gentile in composition and character.

I go into such detail simply because such a background seems to be necessary in order to explain key features in the letter as a whole: particularly the early emphasis that the gospel is 'for Jew first but also for Greek' (especially 1:16), and the repeated warning later against Christian Gentiles adopting airs of superiority over Christian Jews (especially 11:17–24). But even more necessary is such a background to explain the issues and problems addressed in 14:1–15:6, as we shall now see.

3.   What was at issue in Rom. 14:1–15:6?

The issue is briefly stated in the second verse: 'Someone has faith to eat everything; but the weak person eats only vegetables' (14:2). This immediately evokes echoes of modern disagreements about vegetarianism and the right to eat meat. And at once modern concern about individual liberties comes into play. Have not individuals the right, the liberty, to eat meat if they so choose, or to abstain from eating meat if they so choose? Is this what the issue addressed by Paul was about? The answer is No! And the danger is that by thus modernizing the issue and fitting it into the agenda of the modern liberal society we miss the heart of what was at stake for Paul and the implications for Christian liberty. So, what was the issue?[3]

Most, but by no means all, agree that the issue focusses on the Jewish food laws. The practice of vegetarianism for religious or philosophic reasons was quite well known in the ancient world, and on the basis of this fact some have argued that those to whom Paul refers as 'the weak' were Gentile Christians still influenced by their previous beliefs and practices within pagan and mystery religions. But Jewish dietary laws must be in view in Rom. 14 in at least a strong degree.

For one thing, as we have just seen, the Jewish context of Christian beginnings in Rome, and the sustained Jew/Greek, Jew/Gentile motif in the letter itself, point strongly to that conclusion. More significant, however, is the language Paul uses in the discussion of the problem in Rom. 14. In particular, in verse 14 he speaks of things (here meaning food) that are 'unclean'. The word in Greek means simply 'common, ordinary' (*koinos*). The sense 'profane or unclean' derives entirely from the use of *koinos* as the equivalent of the cultic terms in Hebrew *tame'* or *hol* ('unclean or profane'), an equivalence only explicit in our sources subsequent to the LXX rendering of the OT, but clearly evident in the increasing purity concerns of the Maccabean and post-Maccabean period. There are no real parallels in non-Jewish Greek. Almost certainly,

---

3 For fuller details again see my *Romans* pp. 799–802.

then, the issue within the Christian house groups in Rome focussed on the Jewish distinction between clean and unclean food. This is borne out by verse 20, where it is clear that the opposite of *koinos* is *katharos*, 'clean', for the distinction *katharos/akatharos*, 'clean/ unclean' is regularly used in the LXX for the distinction between clean and unclean foods.

What we now need to understand is just how important were the Jewish food laws for Jewish self-understanding. The point is not simply that the laws about clean and unclean food were clearly stated in the Torah, as they are (Lev. 11 and Deut. 14). More to the point is the fact that these laws had become a test-case of Jewish identity and Jewish loyalty to the covenant God had made with Israel, and so a test-case also of loyalty to the covenant God of Israel. The point is well exemplified in the account of the Maccabean crisis in 1 Macc. 1:62–63:

> Many in Israel stood firm and were resolved in their hearts not to eat unclean food. They chose to die rather than to be defiled by food or to profane the holy covenant; and they did die.

It was precisely the Syrian attempt to eliminate this distinctively Jewish practice which brought the Jewish dietary laws to such prominence and made them such a clear test-case – quite literally a matter of life and death.

This sense that observance of the food laws was crucial to Jewish identity, a fundamental principle which could not be compromised without abandoning Israel's covenant and Israel's God, was strongly sustained during the following two centuries. We can see this in the series of popular accounts of Jewish heroes which come from the Maccabean and post-Maccabean period. Daniel is presented as one who was favoured by God precisely because he refused the food of Gentiles and ate only vegetables and drank only water (Dan. 1:12). It is the same with Tobit (Tob. 1:10–13) and Judith (Judith 12:2) and Esther (in the Additions to Esther 14:17) and Joseph (in the romance *Joseph and Asenath* 7:1 and 8:5). In all these accounts the Jewish ideal man and ideal woman were being presented, and in every case a central feature of the presentation was their firm, principled stand on the issue of food laws – the unyielding refusal to eat anything that was unclean.

The problems this caused for infant Christianity are also clearly evident elsewhere in the NT. For Christianity, as I need not remind you, began within second Temple Judaism and was a purely Jewish phenomenon to start with. It was the incoming of Gentiles which posed the questions which racked first generation Christianity: does the conversion of so many Gentiles change the character of the new movement, or does it remain a characteristically Jewish affair, that is, a movement *within* second Temple Judaism, and so a movement operating within the terms of the covenant which governed the people of God? And, not unexpectedly, one of the points at which the issue came to sharpest focus was the food laws. Are the food laws still as fundamental to Jewish and covenant identity?

We recall Peter's protest on the rooftop at Joppa, prior to his encounter with Cornelius, the Roman centurion. Confronted with a large table cloth containing all kinds of animals and reptiles and birds, and bidden by a heavenly voice to 'Rise, kill and eat', Peter is represented as replying with horror, 'No, Lord; for I have never eaten anything that is common or unclean' (Acts 10:11–16; 11:5–10). Even if Peter's initial opposition has been heightened in order to increase the drama of the breakthrough with Cornelius, the centrality of the issue is nevertheless underlined: even a Jew who had followed Jesus and believed in him as Messiah and Lord still saw observance of the laws of clean and unclean as fundamental to his religious practice and identity.

The same point is evident in the Antioch incident which Paul narrates in Gal. 2:11–14. Although Peter and the other Christian Jews at Antioch had been willing to compromise in their observance of the food laws in some degree, when 'certain (unnamed individuals) came from James' in Jerusalem, they all, to a man, it would appear, withdrew from table-fellowship with the Christian Gentiles. Again the centrality and sensitivity of the issue is clear. The Christians from Jerusalem simply could not accept that as Christians they themselves, and other Christian Jews too, should eat with Gentiles in such blatant disregard for the dietary rules which were so fundamental to covenant identity and covenant belonging. And this viewpoint prevailed throughout the Christian Jewish community in Antioch, even though they had previously sat looser to the food laws, even including Peter and Barnabas. Quite clearly, strong chords of ethnic and religious loyalty could be and were being struck and with remarkably unanimous effect.

Evidently the same issues and same fundamental principles were at stake among the Roman Christians too. Whether it was simply a matter of the law of clean and unclean we do not know. These laws did not in fact require vegetarianism as such. Other dimensions of the issue could also have been in play, in particular, the kosher laws, requiring the blood to be properly drained from animals. These required special slaughtering facilities, and Jews might have been unwilling to draw attention to themselves in the capital city by asking for these facilities, when the implementation of Claudius's decree was still of recent memory; to abstain from meat altogether was one way to avoid that dilemma. In addition, there was the fear of meat contaminated by idolatry, that is, by its use in sacrifices in the Roman temples; this was certainly the main problem for the Christians in Corinth, and may have been in the background here. Again, total avoidance of meat was an obvious solution to that problem. Be that as it may, it was the issue of clean and unclean foods which was at the heart of the problems addressed by Paul in Rom. 14, as the centrality of the terms 'unclean' and 'clean' in the argument of Rom. 14 clearly indicates. And it is precisely that issue which would set all the warning bells jangling in the minds of Roman Jews who saw themselves as loyal members of the covenant people.[4]

In short, the importance of the issue at stake in Rom. 14:1–15:6 can hardly be exaggerated. It was no mere issue of irrational food taboos, or of minor questions or of non-essentials, as some commentators have maintained. It was an issue of fundamental definition. What *is* this new movement? What is Christianity? For many Jews their very identity was inextricably bound up with the continued observance of the laws of clean and unclean. To breach these laws would have been an act of profound and decisive disloyalty to everything which they and their people and their religion had stood for hitherto. For such Christian Jews it was virtually inconceivable that followers of Messiah Jesus should sit lightly to laws which were so clearly set out in scripture and which had been such clear-cut test-cases for religious faithfulness and covenant loyalty in the previous two and a half centuries. To abandon the food laws would be to trample on and disown the blood of the martyrs – ever a potent, even inflammatory consideration in controversies where feelings ran deep. Surely, belief in Jesus as

---

4 We have no time to go into the further aspect of the problem indicated in 14.5–6 (whether some days were more important than others); see further again my *Romans* pp. 804–6. It is evident from the passage, however, that the principal issue is the question of clean and unclean food.

Messiah could not require such apostasy – apostasy in matters so clearly laid down in scripture and so clearly affirmed by divine providence in the history of Israel.

That was the issue and its seriousness, at least as seen from the side of traditional Jewish loyalties. It is with reference to this issue and these concerns that Paul sets out a charter for Christian liberty in community.

4. The parties involved

Paul begins by identifying two parties who clearly had a stake in the issue causing some dissension among the Roman Christians – Rom. 14:1–2:

> 1Welcome the one who is weak in faith, though not with a view to settling disputes. 2Someone has faith to eat everything; but the weak person eats only vegetables.

One party consists of those who are 'weak in faith'; the other consists of those first addressed, those whom Paul urges to welcome the weak. The 'weak in faith' are further identified as those who 'eat only vegetables'. Presumably the others are those who have 'faith to eat everything'; they have faith which the 'weak' lack. The latter are not more closely identified at this point, but since they are contrasted with the 'weak in faith', the implication is that they are 'strong in faith' – an implication borne out in 15:1 where Paul speaks explicitly of 'the strong': 'we the strong ought to support the weaknesses of those without strength.' So in analyzing Paul's teaching on this subject we may speak simply of the 'weak' and the 'strong' and be confident that we are using Paul's terms and not some straw men of our own construction.

Who were the weak and who were the strong? Given that the issue was primarily one of the Jewish food laws, and given the sensitivities on this issue just outlined, the most obvious answer is that the weak were Christian Jews – Jews, who, like Peter before his vision at Joppa, or like Peter after the incident at Antioch, felt it essential to continue to maintain their Jewish identity by continuing to observe the Jewish food laws. We need not assume that this was the stand taken by all the Christian Jews in Rome: Paul himself was a Jew and he took a different position; and no doubt there were others like him, Priscilla and Aquila, for example, whose practice was similar to Paul's. Nor need we confine the ranks of the 'weak' to Jews. Most of the earliest Gentile converts to faith in Messiah Jesus almost certainly came through the synagogue; they had been attracted first to the Jewish way of life, as God-fearers or proselytes, before being attracted by the good news of Jesus. And one of the things which had attracted many of them would have been the Jewish dietary laws. We can well imagine, on the basis of many parallels, that there were Gentiles who, with the zeal of converts, had become passionate in their practice of such Jewish distinctives as the food laws, and who saw their faith in Messiah Jesus simply as an extension or fuller definition of their earlier conversion to the religion of Jesus.

Paul also describes them as 'weak in faith'. He has used the same phrase earlier in his description of Abraham in chapter 4, so we can be fairly sure of what he means. Abraham had been promised a son when he and his wife were far beyond child-bearing age. 'Against hope, in hope "he believed" ' (Gen. 15:6) God's promise.

> He did not become weak in faith by considering his own body, already dead . . . or the deadness of Sarah's womb. He did not doubt the promise of God in disbelief, but was strengthened in faith, giving glory to God, being, fully convinced that what God had promised he was able to do (Rom 4:18–21).

The point is clear: to be 'weak in faith' is to fail to trust God completely and without qualification. Abraham had nothing else to rely on, no ground of hope, no reason for confidence other than God's promise. That was the strength of his faith; there was nothing else he could do except trust God alone. To be weak in faith, then, is *to trust in something other than God, or something in addition to God.* In terms of Rom. 14, that must mean, to trust in God *plus* observance of the food laws, to make trust in God *dependent* on observance of such practices, a trust in God which leans on the crutches of particular rules or customs and not on God alone, *as though there could be no real trust without such observances.* Linking this in to the previous lecture, we may characterize weakness in faith as failure to realize and live out liberty from the law, failure to realize that the life of the Spirit need no longer necessarily be restricted within the limitations of traditional and distinctive Jewish customs.

The 'strong', in contrast, would be those Christian Jews and Gentiles who saw the food laws as no more, or no more necessarily binding on believers in Messiah Jesus. They were those, in Paul's terms, who saw trust in God and his Messiah as the sole necessary and sufficient condition for relation with God through his Messiah. They were strong *in faith.*

It is important to note at once that Paul counts himself as one of 'the strong' ('we the strong' – 15.1). In addition the very terminology betrays the perspective of 'the strong': it is those who think themselves 'strong' who regard others as 'weak'; the 'weak' is hardly a self-chosen designation of those so designated. Would the weak have so regarded themselves? Hardly. On the contrary, they would probably have regarded themselves as 'strong' – strong in defence of the scriptural laws and traditions of Israel, strong in defence of the God-given practices of piety for which their fathers and the noble army of martyrs had died. The issue, I repeat, was no secondary or minor matter, but a fundamental difference of perspective.

We have thus hardly begun to open up the passage and it is already clear that it may provide an illustration of wider relevance. For the clash of opinions so far described is typical of the divisions which have so often racked Christians since then. Need I remind you of the old disputes over the Lord's Supper, eucharist or mass, over episcopacy, over Sunday observance, or today over homosexuality, abortion and the ordination of women. All of these have seemed to the combatants equally as fundamental and fully as important as the issue in Rom. 14. In broad terms we might say it is the clash of those who hold more firmly to traditional beliefs and practices, and those who want to sit more loose to such beliefs and practices – in this case the traditional beliefs and practices of God-given instruction refined in the fire of persecution and martyrdom. Can we even define it in more general terms as the clash between conservative and liberal? That may impose too simple a stereotype on the issue in Rom. 14, but at least it would remind us that for one party at least, the issue is one of liberty. Whatever terms we use, however, the potential value of the passage is in how Paul handles the issue. How then does Paul define and defend Christian liberty in the context of a community divided on matters regarded by one of the parties at least as of fundamental importance?

5. The threat to Christian community

Paul begins by defining the dangers which the issue of food laws posed to the Christian groups in Rome, the threat to the Christian community made up of the various house churches in Rome. 'Welcome the one who is weak in faith', he urges immediately – 'welcome' in the sense of receive or accept into one's society, home or circle of acquaintances. Evidently there was a danger that the more traditionalist Christian Jews would not be accepted into the house churches at Rome. We have already speculated that this exhortation reflects the situation where Roman Christianity had become more Gentile in number and character following the expulsion of Christian Jews like Priscilla and Aquila six or so years earlier, and where Christian Jews were beginning to return to Rome following the lapse of Claudius's edict. Given the issue of food laws and Jewish sensitivities on the subject, we can also understand why predominantly Gentile Christian groups in Rome might be unwilling to accept more conservative Christian Jews in view of their various scruples over the food laws, with all that that entailed for their mutual table-fellowship, Sunday by Sunday, or whenever they met and ate together.

The exhortation is addressed initially to the strong (14:1). But in 15:7, in summing up the plea of 14:1–15:6, Paul broadens it out to all: 'Therefore, welcome one another, as Christ also welcomed you'. So the challenge is one of mutual acceptance. And the threat to community is that *one group is unwilling to accept the other*.

14:3 gives the point still sharper definition: 'Let the one who eats not despise the one who does not eat, and let not the one who does not eat pass judgment on the one who eats, for God has welcomed him.' The language is very striking and reveals a penetrating insight on Paul's part into the psychology of the groups involved. The one who eats (the strong) will be tempted to 'despise', to hold in contempt those who do not eat (the weak). This, we may say, is the characteristic temptation for those who regard themselves as 'strong', namely, to *despise* those whom they regard as 'weak'.

The liberal in his broadmindedness despises the conservative for his narrowness and legalistic scruples (as so perceived by the liberal). On the other hand, the one who does not eat (the weak) will be tempted to 'pass judgment on', to condemn those who do eat, who ignore the food laws. This is the language which Paul had used at the beginning of Rom. 2 – the Jewish interlocutor who condemns the typically Gentile sins described in chapter 1, confident that he himself stands secure in his own covenant relation with God. It is equally clear, both from chapter 2 and from the following verses in chapter 14, that the weak condemns the strong because he assumes that God also condemns them (14:4, 10). This, we may say, is the characteristic temptation of the more conservative, namely, to *condemn* the more liberal: they are conservative on such issues because they are convinced this is what God requires; they condemn more liberal practices because they assume that God does so.

The threat to Christian community is therefore clear. One section actually questions the Christian standing of another. Their definition of what Christianity is, and what it means to be a Christian, is tighter, includes more elements among the fundamentals of the faith. Since the others do not agree that food laws are among the fundamentals and act in disregard of them the conclusion is inescapable: those who disregard God's laws cannot be acceptable to the God who laid down these laws; they are no Christians. Clearly, when one party holds such an opinion of others there can be no real communion between them. But there is an equal danger on the other side: that the liberals fail to respect the more conservative, treat their views dismissively, even derisively. Clearly, when there is such lack of genuine respect one for the other, there can be no communion between them.

To meet this threat Paul proposes the solution of

Christian liberty. His treatment falls into two parts, when he addresses first predominantly the 'weak' (14:1–12), and then, secondly, the 'strong' (14:13–15:6).

6. The answer of Christian liberty: the appeal to the weak

The main thrust of Paul's exhortation here is given at once (14:1–12):

> 3. . . . Let not the one who does not eat pass judgment on the one who does eat, for God has welcomed him. 4Who are you to condemn the slave of someone else? In relation to his own master he stands or falls. And he shall stand, for his master is able to make him stand. 5. . . Let each be fully convinced in his own mind. 6. . . The one who eats does so to the Lord, for he gives thanks to God; and the one who does not eat does so to the Lord and gives thanks to God. . . . 10So you, why do you judge your brother? Or you, why do you despise your brother? For we shall all stand before the judgment seat of God . . .

Paul's response to the more conservative is, first of all, to challenge the basic assumption which gives rise to the condemnation of the more liberal; that is, to challenge the traditionalists to recognize that Christianity is larger than their definition of it, to recognize that *God* accepts people whose views and practices *they* regard as unacceptable. Paul presses the point with repeated emphasis: 'God has welcomed him . . . he is God's servant . . . he will stand because it is precisely and solely God's prerogative and power to make him stand' (14:3–4). This is the crucial step in Paul's pastoral strategy: to get the more conservative actually to accept that someone who differs from them, and differs in something they regard as fundamental, may nevertheless be acceptable to God and accepted by God; to recognize that they are in danger of falling into the trap of defining God too narrowly, of confining him within the limits of their own convictions, of worshipping a God made in their own image, of dictating to God and setting up their own judgment in place of God's.

Paul's second piece of counsel is that each should be fully convinced in his own mind on such contentious subjects which affected the oneness of the Christian congregations. Each should make up his own mind *for himself.*[5] Strength of personal conviction should not be used to intimidate the other. My conscience is the measure for my own conduct before God; it should not be used as a stick to beat my brother, whose conscience may speak to him differently.[6] Each must weigh such issues before God and reach his own conclusions, even if it means differing, and differing quite sharply from the other. That is what Christian liberty is about, and to abandon that is to destroy Christian liberty. Here, clearly implied, is Paul's firm recognition that Christians will disagree with one another, and on important issues, and yet each can properly be convinced of the rightness of his or her position. Two believers can disagree, *and yet both be right* (that is, accepted by God). Given that we disagree, it is *not* necessary for *you* to be *wrong* in order that *I* should be *right*. There can be legitimate differences, on important matters, and equally held in good faith.

---

5 I follow the gender specific language of the text in order to restate what it says as closely as possible; but Paul's teaching was obviously directed to the whole congregation as each gathered to hear his letter read out to them, and in their ranks were evidently many women including at least some in prominent leadership roles (Rom. 16:3–12).

6 Paul does not use the word 'conscience' in Rom. 14–15, but it is prominent in the parallel treatment of 1 Cor. 8–10 (8:7, 10, 12; 10:25–29), and the importance of acting in accord with one's trust in God and sense of what is acceptable to God is emphasized in Rom. 14:22–23.

Paul was well aware that such liberty of opinion and practice must seem both frightening and threatening to the more conservative. Where will it all end? If the fundamentals for one can be so questioned by the other and yet the other still be counted acceptable, does not that inevitably mean that all fundamentals are open to question and rejection? Is Paul's counsel not a classic example of the slippery slope? – once abandon the fundamentals of the food laws, and there is nothing to prevent a headlong flight from every fundamental; once begin questioning such hallowed dogma and tradition, then it becomes impossible to prevent corrosive liberal scepticism eating into every dogma and tradition. This concern, you will recall, lies at the heart of Newman's rejection of Liberalism. In other terms, does liberty have no limits? How can one prevent acceptable liberty from degenerating into unacceptable license?

It is important to realize, therefore, that Paul is able to assume common, central ground. He takes it for granted that both parties in the dispute will have reached their conclusions *before their common Lord*; he assumes that they each live out their diverse patterns of conduct *in honour of their common Lord and in thankfulness to God*. That is to say, the range of acceptable liberty is restricted to what is appropriate as Christian obedience and as the expression of creaturely dependence on the Creator (cf. 14:6 with 1:21). Only what can be received from God and offered to God in humble thankfulness counts as acceptable Christian conduct. That is the real foundation of Christian liberty in expression of faith and life-style; not the fact of different opinions, but the fact that these different opinions are reached and lived out in humble submissiveness before God as final judge. Whoever can lay just claim to such obedience and hold his or her conduct before Christ in thanksgiving to God should be accepted as a Christian, even if that conduct is controversial or disagreeable to others' conception of discipleship. In the end of the day it is God who determines acceptable conduct, and acceptance by God is the measure of acceptable conduct – nothing less, but nothing more.

Paul's conclusion, then, is clear. Neither of the different groups in Rome has any right either to condemn the other or to make slighting remarks about the other. Each must answer for himself or herself and not for anyone else. Indeed, each will answer for herself or himself in the final judgment (14:10). And one of the things each will have to give account of is precisely such condemnatory or dismissive attitudes to those whom God has accepted. Thus ends the first part of Paul's charter of Christian liberty and mutual tolerance.

7. The answer of Christian liberty: the appeal to the strong

The second part of the appeal is directed to the strong (14:13–15:6). In fact it is the strong who are the main targets of Paul's exhortation throughout, so that his counsel is more scattered. But it can be summed up under three points.

First, the liberty of the strong is and can only be based on *faith*. This is simply to reaffirm the point already made – the relation of trust in God through Christ is what determines acceptable conduct. But Paul reasserts the point more than once in the second half of chapter 14. He states his own position clearly, unequivocally siding with the strong – 'I know and am convinced in the Lord Jesus that nothing is unclean in itself (14:14). The fact that his conviction has been reached and is maintained 'in the Lord Jesus' is the crucial factor; very likely also he is deliberately referring in this allusive way to Jesus' own teaching on clean and unclean.[7] In other words, Paul takes care to root the authority for his views and conduct both in the Jesus tradition and in his personal relationship with Christ. Hence also the emphasis of verse 18 — it is 'he who serves the Christ in this (who) is pleasing to God'. And in the last two verses he emphasizes even more strongly that Christian conduct must emerge out of faith and be an expression of that same fundamental trust in God, otherwise the conduct is sin: indeed 'everything which is not of faith is sin' (14:23). That is a principle which, rightly applied, should help prevent the liberty of the weak degenerating into legalism and the liberty of the strong degenerating into license.

Second, the more liberal should recognize the scruples of the more conservative and respect them as true brothers and sisters in the Lord. Just as the more conservative must truly accept and not condemn the more liberal, so the more liberal must truly accept and not despise the more conservative. The antidote and antithesis to both diseases is genuine acceptance of and respect for the integrity of the other. Again the point is made several times. The strong are to welcome those who are weak in faith, 'though not with a view to settling disputes' (14:1). The zeal of the liberals to instruct and 'enlighten' their more conservative fellow Christians has to be curbed. Paul of course hopes to do a bit of instructing in his letter; but he is quite clear that the weak should be accepted just as they are and not in any provisional or conditional sense. Similarly at the other end of the chapter he counsels his readers to keep their own convictions on such issues to themselves

---

7 See e.g. my 'Jesus and Ritual Purity: A Study of the Tradition-History of Mark 7.15', *Jesus, Paul and the Law* (London: SPCK/Louisville: Westminster, 1990) pp. 37–60; also 'Jesus Tradition in Paul', *Studying the Historical Jesus: Evaluations of the State of Current Research*, ed. B. D. Chilton & C. A. Evans (Leiden: Brill, 1994).

before God (14:22). If the more conservative should not beat others over the head with their scruples, neither should the more liberal constantly push their liberal views and practice in front of the more conservative.

So too in verse 14, having stated his own conviction about clean and unclean, Paul adds, 'but to the one who reckons something unclean, to that person it is unclean'. And he goes on to recognize that such convictions can be so deeply rooted that a brother might be 'deeply upset on account of food', might indeed be 'destroyed' by someone's more liberal practice on food matters (14:15–16). Paul here clearly wants to inculcate in his readers a genuine sensitivity to and sympathy for the conservative minority. He recognizes that they are in a real and not merely imaginary danger. Without their intending it to be so, the conduct of the liberal majority might be deeply hurtful and genuinely damaging to those whose identity was still largely shaped by Jewish traditional convictions and customs.[8] So integral to covenant loyalty had been the practice of the food laws that Christian Jews could still feel themselves excluded from the covenant, cut off from grace by disobedience at this point. In classic liberal terms, Paul pleads with his own passion for the right of the more conservative to continue to maintain their conservative views and to be accepted as they are.

Third, and the main emphasis, Paul exhorts the more liberal always to condition the expression of their liberty by love for the other, including particularly the more conservative other.

> 13Let us therefore ... decide not to put an occasion for offense or downfall in the brother's way. ...

---

8 But this point should not be taken out of context, as is often done in formulating the principle of 'the weaker brother'.

15For if your brother is deeply upset on account of food, you are no longer conducting yourself in terms of love. . . . 21It is a fine thing not to eat meat or drink wine nor anything by which your brother stumbles. . . . 15.1We the strong ought to support the weaknesses of those without strength, and not to please ourselves. 2Let us each please his neighbour with a view to what is good, for upbuilding. 3For the Christ too did not please himself . . .

The point is clear: the more liberal must take into account not only their own convictions in determining their actual conduct, but also the way their conduct affects their more conservative fellow Christians. The pattern here is Christ: he adapted his own freedom and conduct to the needs of his neighbour; he did not seek simply to please himself. The implications for those who determine their convictions 'in Christ' (14:14) and who seek to serve Christ (14:18) are clear. At this point, naturally, we can link back into what emerged from the second lecture and not least the paradox of a liberty which takes the freely chosen service of the slave as its model (e.g. Rom. 15:1–8; Phil. 2:5–7).[9]

In the same spirit, it is precisely the strong whom Paul reminds that 'the kingdom of God is not a matter of eating and drinking, but of righteousness, peace and joy in the Holy Spirit' (14:17). So far as the weak are concerned, the kingdom of God may indeed still be bound up with eating and drinking; it is the strong who affirm the claim of Christian liberty that continued observance of the clean and unclean laws is no longer a condition of participating in the inheritance of God's kingdom. The point is that that liberty cuts both ways – if it is genuine liberty, it is liberty both to observe the

---

9 We do not have time to develop the point in Rom. 14:16 and 18 that an important factor influencing patterns of conduct should also be the impact of that conduct on others outside the church.

food laws, and liberty from the food laws. If observance of the Jewish food laws no longer makes any difference to participation in God's kingdom, then it doesn't matter that much whether the food laws are observed or not. The ritual moment is just not that important. Consequently the true test of the liberal's liberty is whether he is willing to restrict it; only when it is liberty to deny oneself and not just liberty to please oneself can it be counted Christian liberty. Where the fundamental principle of faith does not point to a clear course of conduct, then it is love of neighbour which must shape the practice of liberty.

There is of course a problem here, analogous to the problem which follows from Paul's counsel to the weak. As we already noted, the weak would naturally be nervous lest slipping the reins on liberty resulted in a headlong rush into license. But so would the strong be nervous lest a willingness to restrict their liberty become a sop to legalism. Calvin long ago recognized the problem when he distinguished the weak from the Pharisee, understanding the latter as the type of legalism. His solution was neatly expressed: 'we will so temper the use of our liberty as to make it yield to the ignorance of weak brethren, but not to the austerity of Pharisees' (*Institutes* 3.19.11).

Paul was evidently conscious of the need for some similar nuances. So at the end of chapter 14 he makes it clear that he had in mind real and not imagined damage done to the weak – an actual stumble and fall (14:13, 20, 21), a real 'hurt' (14:15), final 'destruction' (14:15, 20) – what Calvin distinguishes in the same passage as offence given and not simply offence taken. So in 14:23 the danger to the conservative arises not merely from seeing the liberal doing something of which the conservative disapproves, but from being forced (by example or social pressure) to act against his or her convictions – the damage in view is not that of being offended by *other people's* eating unclean food, but that of *actually eating unclean food themselves* despite all their doubts and convictions. Paul, in other words, has no intention of encouraging the weak to exercise undue pressure on their own behalf – to blackmail the strong by professing grief or hurt at the conduct of the strong. For liberty to be seriously curtailed, it would not be sufficient that the more conservative disapprove of the more liberal; Paul has in mind only situations where the conservatives' trust in God is actually undermined by the action of the more liberated – their trust in God undermined, not just their scruples.

In short, Christian liberty must be defended against the condemnatory attitude of the weak as much as against the disdainful self-indulgence of the strong (14:3). In calling for the more liberal to condition their liberty by sensitive concern for the more conservative, Paul does not mean that they should abandon their liberty altogether. The unconditional character of faith must be allowed to come to expression in liberty; the concern for another which overrestricts liberty is a cheap love which damages faith as well. The balance of faith, liberty and love must be maintained, however difficult.

8. Conclusions

We can thus sum up Paul's teaching on Christian liberty and community diagramatically.

THE SPECTRUM OF CHRISTIAN LIBERTY
conditioned by LOVE

LICENSE   s t r o n g   w e a k   LEGALISM

arising from FAITH

It is important to recognize in summary (1) that Christian liberty is a spectrum, which contains a diversity of expressions of faith in word and practice; (2) that the spectrum of liberty in any (Christian) group will always include those who are more conservative and those who are more liberal; (3) that liberty will always be threatened from within a community by failure of all those who are members of the community truly to respect the others, the more conservative being tempted to condemn the more liberal, the more liberal to despise the more conservative; (4) that liberty will always be threatened from without, at either end of that spectrum by the weak lapsing into the legalism of overscrupulousness and the strong lapsing into the license of self-pleasing; (5) that Christian liberty as such can exist only insofar as it emerges out of and is an expression of faith in Christ;[10] and (6) that it can be sustained only within the spectrum which is any church if it is conditioned by love. It is precisely this love of neighbour, we should note, which prevents the liberty of the strong becoming the license of the self-pleasing.

Here then is a very different view of liberty and society from that of Mill. For Mill, liberty meant essentially liberty *from* society – *laissez faire*, hands off. The liberty of the individual could be restricted only when it was interfering with the liberty of others. But this, as we already noted, is the plea of the elite, able to flourish in just such a society; in terms of the discussion of this chapter, it is the plea of the strong insufficiently concerned for the weak. The Pauline view of society is partly the same, but significantly different. It shares a similar concern for liberty – indeed, not just the freedom of the minority over against the majority, but also the freedom of the majority from the crippling scruples of the illiberal minority. But the Pauline view

---

10 Cf. this observation with the passage quoted from Hayek on p. 24.

of liberty and society is different from that of Mill in
one crucial respect – in the strong emphasis Paul places
on the responsibility of the more liberal to *limit* their
freedom for the sake of those who do not share their
views. This is what marks Paul's view off from that of
Mill. For Paul, liberty is liberty *in* society, as part of
society, a liberty which is conditioned for the sake of
community, a liberty which functions not simply as
freedom of the individual, but in and as responsibility
towards society.

In fact, Paul's understanding of liberty and its
outworking is simply an expression of his understanding of community on the analogy of the human body,
and of Christian community as the body of Christ
(Rom. 12:3–8; 1 Cor. 12). For fundamental to that
vision of community is not simply the recognition that
diversity of its members is indispensable – that is
something on which Mill agrees. But that diversity of
its members is indispensable to its *unity*. Paul insists on
recognition and full acceptance of diversity, because it
is the different functions of the many members which
makes up the oneness of the body; the body cannot
exist as a body, as one body, without that diversity. But
that also means, and this again is where Paul differs
from Mill, that the diversity exists not for itself, or on
behalf of indomitable individualism, independent of
society, but exists on behalf of society, *for* society. The
point is that society can be sustained as one only where
there is genuine respect one for another among its
diverse members, only where there is the shared
sympathy that comes from being part of the *one*
society, only where there is voluntary restraint on the
part of the individual for the sake of that society.

This is a vision which can apply to liberty and
society as a whole, and can be adapted to the problem
of the liberty of minorities in terms indicated by the
quotation from Hayek at the end of the first lecture.

But Christian liberty in particular stresses also the importance of resources and enabling beyond that of the merely human – not just 'deeply ingrained moral beliefs', but faith, dependence on divine enabling for aspirations which otherwise succumb to human corruption and self-pleasing, the enabling of the Spirit. And, not least, the example and pattern of Christ, who constantly reminds us by life and word that Christian freedom is not reducible to freedom to choose, but in the end is nothing if it is not freedom to love the neighbour, warts and all, differences and all. Only such liberty, growing from faith and expressed through love is sufficient to sustain true community.

Afterword

In Dostoevsky's *The Brothers Karamazov*, there is a famous chapter entitled 'The Grand Inquisitor'. In it Dostoevsky imagines that Jesus returned to earth and visited Seville during the time of the Inquisition. He was arrested and brought before the Grand Inquisitor, and the resulting interrogation, or rather monologue by the Grand Inquisitor forms the substance of the chapter.

The main theme of the Grand Inquisitor's examination is freedom. Jesus, in refusing to work miracles (turning stones into bread) which would have won him a following, put freedom of faith higher than miracle. It was this freedom he came to bring. But this freedom is a troublesome thing, which people will willingly surrender in exchange for bread. 'Man, so long as he remains free, has no more constant and agonizing anxiety than to find as quickly as possible someone to worship ... even when the gods have vanished from the earth they will prostrate themselves before idols just the same ... Man has no more agonizing anxiety than to find someone to whom he can hand over with all speed the gift of freedom with which the unhappy creature is born. ... There is nothing more alluring to man than this freedom of conscience, but there is nothing more tormenting, either'.

The drift of the Grand Inquisitor's speech is that the Church recognized that freedom only makes for unhappiness and gave man what he really wants – the safety and security which comes with miracle, mystery and authority. 'We have corrected your great work', says the Grand Inquisitor to the silent prisoner, 'and based it on miracle, mystery and authority. And men rejoiced that they were once more led like sheep and that the terrible gift which had brought them so much suffering had at last been lifted from their hearts'. The burden of the Grand Inquisitor's charge against Jesus is that Jesus himself with his message of freedom threatens this peaceful outcome. 'With us, however, all will be happy and will no longer rise in rebellion nor exterminate one another, as they do everywhere under your freedom. Oh, we will convince them that only then will they become free when they have resigned their freedom to us and have submitted to us'.

Dostoevsky brings a sharp eye to the problem of liberty – that it is troublesome, that it can lead to war and suffering. But the solution of the Grand Inquisitor is a tight control by the few who keep the masses in infantile subjection. And Dostoevsky rightly sees that the life of faith lived by and called for by Jesus breaks through such manipulation and control. The message is poignantly apposite in a day when the nations of the former Communist empire of eastern Europe are struggling to control the freedom which they greeted with such joy only a few years ago, and will continue to be apposite for many Christians struggling free from the bonds of an overprescriptive tutelage.

Is the Grand Inquisitor right in presenting the liberty of Jesus as too frightening for most people? Is he right that the only alternative is to hand over liberty to some authoritative figure or institution? Certainly the spirit of freedom will always revolt and rise against such manipulation and control and oppression. And, sadly, the exultation of the moment of liberation will again and again be soured by excesses and power struggles of the too ambitious or in pursuit of some pure ideal. How tragic that the precious gift of liberty should be so threatening that it gives such scope to renewed authoritarianism, and so undisciplined that it confirms those who fear it in their prejudices. Christian liberty in fact recognizes both dangers, and offers both the Spirit of liberty and the necessary checks and balances of community belonging and community obligation. The 'freedom of Jesus' is something that no Christian need or should fear, a freedom in a growing maturity, where love is the inspiring but also the controlling force – love such as Jesus himself expressed in life and death.

Jesus said, 'If you continue in my word, you are truly my disciples, and you will know the truth, and the truth will make you free. . . . So if the Son makes you free, you will be free indeed' (John 8:31–32,36).

Index of Biblical References

Index of Authors

Index of Subjects